October 2044

With hope for a better tomorrow

P.H. Mattsson

This book is a translated version of the Swedish book titled *Oktober 2044: Med hopp om en bättre morgondag*, written by the same author 2023-2024.

Table of Contents

CHAPTER 1

October 24, 2044

"No, no … please … no … stop! Don't touch my head! It feels like it's about to explode. Ouch! Please … no … no!"

"Sorry, I have to. I'm trying to stop a bleeding from your forehead, but I can't see anything in this total darkness. I'll have to feel my way with my hands. Stay still!"

"Who are you? What happened? Ouch!"

"I'll answer all your questions … but later. Right now, it'll have to wait. I need to focus on what I'm doing. Stay still and try to stay calm. I can feel blood seeping out right above your right eye, but I don't think you're bleeding anywhere else, at least not that I've found with my hands."

"Above my right eye? I don't have any eyes, you know that, right? My eyes were shot out many years ago."

"Yes, I know. Since we now have 2044, it must have been about 20 years since that happened."

"Is it the year 2044 now? I can't believe it! Time has really flown."

"So you didn't know what year we are in? You have really been completely isolated from the outside world."

"Hmm … "

"Stay still, now I really need to focus on the wound above your right ... "

"You can say *'above the right eye socket'*. Eye sockets, completely empty eye sockets, that's what I have. There are no eyes, they're gone."

"I think I've got the wound under control. It doesn't seem that big, but it's still bleeding a lot."

"Ouch ... can't you just tell me what happened and who you are? "

"You've been unconscious for about 15-20 minutes, and you've probably got a pretty bad concussion. I guess your head hit something inside the elevator when it suddenly stopped. It was a really hard stop, and you didn't have a seatbelt on."

"What ... what elevator ... and seatbelts in an elevator? I don't get it! What happened? Who are you? Where are we? Ouch ... my head is pounding and hurting so badly."

"Calm down, I'll tell you. It seems like the concussion has given you a memory gap, a temporary memory loss. I'll explain what happened ... as much as I know ... but right now, I need to stop the bleeding. I'm going to put a bandage around your head. I tore strips from my shirt."

"Aren't you done yet?"

"There, now I think I've tied a knot that should hold the bandage in place. Don't tear it off. Try to relax. I'll tell you what happened and who I am soon ... but rest for a little while first."

"Okay ... I'll try ... to rest ... for a bit. Ugh, I feel a little nauseous ... and tired ... "

CHAPTER 2

"Hmm ... "

"Rashid, are you awake? How are you feeling? I think you've been asleep for a couple of hours."

"Oh, you know my name. Have we met before?"

"No, this morning was the first time, but I've been told a lot about you. I've also read some things written about you in various places. Is your head feeling better? You were in a lot of pain earlier."

"Mmm … I think so … I still have some pain, but that pounding ache is gone."

"Good! I think the bleeding has stopped, but the bandage should probably stay on for a while. Try not to touch it."

"I taste blood in my mouth."

"Not surprising. A lot of blood could've run down from your forehead. You may have also bitten your tongue or the inside of your cheek in the fall. That happened to me once when I crashed my bike when I was a kid."

"You said someone told you who I am, but I know nothing about you ... that doesn't seem fair. Who told you about me, and what did they say?"

"My cousin told me quite a bit."

"Your cousin? How does he know anything about me?"

"My cousin isn't a '*he*'. Her name is Sara, and she works as a guard here at the prison."

"Sara! She's great. She's kind and seems to understand my situation better than the others who work here."

"I'm glad you're talking to me now. I've read in some reports that you haven't been able to communicate at all since you were shot in the head. One report even said that the brain damage caused you to suffer from a severe form of aphasia, and whenever someone tried to speak to you, you would just cover your ears and scream. It seems you've been cut off from all forms of human communication during your more than 20 years here at the prison, up until recently ... "

"Has Sara been gossiping?"

"Gossiping about what?"

"Ah, nothing. Is it still total darkness where we are?"

"Yes, we're in an underground bunker, and it seems there's no working lighting. I've felt along the walls and found a couple of switches, but none of them worked. I also haven't found any remote control or anything that could turn on the lights. I've even tried some common voice commands. Nothing worked."

"Don't you have a cell phone or a smartphone with a flashlight?"

"Cell phone or smartphone? It's been a long time since I've heard those words. Nowadays, everyone says *Communicator* or *ComU*. Sure, I have a ComU with a light function, but it's completely dead. Nothing on my ComU works, and that's never happened before. The screens are completely dead. It doesn't respond to my voice commands, gestures, or pressing anywhere. Nothing works, not even the light function."

"Is the battery dead?"

"It's worse than that. It has an emergency charger built in. There's a small scroll wheel in one corner that lets you manually charge the phone by rolling the wheel back and forth on a flat surface. I tried for a long time on the floor while you were sleeping, but it didn't work. I think it's damaged somehow. It's totally busted!"

"ComU? Why weren't the old names good enough?"

"A ComU has functionality that's light years ahead of what the old devices could do. A new name was needed."

"A lot of new features? You'll have to tell me more about that. It sounds really interesting."

"Sure, but it might take a while. We'll get to that later."

"Hey, I need to use the restroom. Is there one?"

"Yes, it's nearby. I'll guide you there. It's an old-fashioned toilet with a handle you lift to flush water. I've tried it, and the flush works. But there's no bidet function or warm air dryer. Apparently, you're supposed to wipe yourself with toilet paper like in the old days. There's a roll hanging on the wall next to the toilet. I also found some extra rolls in packages under the sink, which is also an older model. To get water from the faucet, you lift a lever, but it only gives cold water no matter how I move the lever. It doesn't have voice control, at least not one that responds to me, but at least water comes out. I let it run for a while when I tested it, and I even tasted a little from my cupped hand. It tasted okay. There are also some plastic barrels stacked in a corner of the room."

"Okay."

"Stand up now. I'll help you; I'll lead you to the restroom."

"As someone who's blind, I'm used to getting around in total darkness, so maybe I should be the one leading you if you just show me which way to go."

"This time, I think it's better if I lead you. Let's go."

"Thanks, but wow, you're shaking. What's wrong? Are you not feeling well?"

"We're close to the restroom now, just a few more steps. Here's the door. You can probably handle things yourself inside. How's the nausea? Do you need to throw up?"

"No, and I'll be fine. It's just normal needs I need to take care of ... *number one* and *number two*. I'll see you soon."

CHAPTER 3

"Rashid, did everything go okay in the restroom?"

"Yes ... and I used the toilet paper sparingly."

"What? Do you think we'll be down here for a long time? Is that why you're rationing the paper?"

"I don't know. What do you think? Will we be down here for long?"

"There's a chance we could be stuck here for quite some time. What if we never get out?"

"Then toilet paper probably won't be our biggest problem. Can you tell me now what exactly happened and who you are? Why do you think we might be stuck down here for a long time?"

"I'll explain, but first, let's sit down in the room next door. There's a table with some chairs. I'll lead you there."

"Thanks, but you're shaking a lot. You're trembling all over. Are you sick? Cold?"

"No, I think it's the shock of what just happened to us. I'm terrified and worried about us, everyone up there ... and the world. I wonder what happened to Sara? Is she alive? Will she come down here soon?"

"You're really scared."

"Yes. Will we make it out of here alive? Right now, the situation feels like a big question mark, a huge frightening question mark. But you, Rashid, seem so calm. Aren't you scared? Your voice sounds so steady."

"My life has been full of misery, terrible events, and dangerous situations. I guess I've become hardened. Besides, darkness and being locked up have become normal for me. I stopped worrying about things a long time ago. Things will happen as they happen, and I've never had any control over what's going to happen."

"Alright, we've reached the table. Sit down on this chair. I think we're in some kind of combined meeting room and break room. There's a small kitchenette at one end of the room, to the left when you walk in. I've already scoped the area a bit, so I can tell you more about what's in the different rooms down here."

"But come on and tell me what happened to us and who you are! What's down here is interesting, but we can talk about that later. Tell me now!"

"Okay, here's the deal. My name is Fredrik Andersson, and I'm an investigative journalist at an agency called *Seven Spades*. It's a journalist bureau that functions somewhat like a news agency."

"*Seven Spades* ... that's a strange name."

"There were seven of us journalists who started the agency together a few years ago. We mostly work on assignments from external clients, mostly here in Sweden, but sometimes we take our own initiatives. Our goal is always to dig for the truth in all the projects we take on, or at least try to get as close to the truth as possible. We see ourselves as truth diggers."

"Aha, that explains the name. But go on, tell me what happened and why you and I are down here. You're dancing around the topic and avoiding my question. Is there a reason you're not telling me?"

"No, not really. I live in Eskilstuna, but I'm originally from a small village in the province of Jämtland, not far from here, just a few miles away. My cousin Sara told me that this prison is going to be shut down soon, and all the inmates will be transferred to other facilities around Sweden and, in some cases, even to other countries. In your case, deportation to Iran or the US is being considered. Sara feels that such a deportation wouldn't be right. She's starting to doubt whether you're guilty of everything you've been accused of. She told me a bit about you at a family gathering we had in Östersund this past summer, and I got interested in your story. Now she wants me, as an investigative journalist, to look into your case to see if everything has really been handled properly, legally speaking."

"Wow, this is all new to me. Oh my God! I didn't know the prison was going to be shut down and that I might be deported. That's the same as a death sentence for me. I've been convicted in Iran for a murder I didn't commit. I'd probably be executed on the spot if that deportation goes through."

"No, you wouldn't be executed if you're sent to Iran because they abolished the death penalty there several years ago. Not a single country in the world has the death penalty anymore. A few years ago, the UN pressured all countries that still had it, and they quickly changed. It only took a few years for all countries to agree."

"Is that really true? The UN has gained that much power? I'm really surprised. All these years, I've been faking being gravely ill and unresponsive because I absolutely didn't want to be sent to Iran. It was a matter of survival for me. But I've also had other reasons for escaping into my own world of fantasy and shutting out everyone and everything around me."

"A lot has changed in the world during the years you've chosen to isolate yourself from reality. The UN today is totally different from the UN we had 20 years ago. The organization has played an enormous role in making the world safer and trying to save humanity from the catastrophe we were quickly heading toward. Their focus has been entirely on preventing wars and putting all resources toward dealing with the dramatic climate changes."

"The UN? The same UN that was so powerless? How in the world has the UN changed so drastically?"

"It'll take some time to explain, but the biggest reason the organization now has such a strong and important role is the terrible climate disasters the world has faced in recent decades. There's been a growing realization that the world must unite and use all available resources together to try to get the climate under control. Plus, I don't think we would've reached that realization without the dramatic developments in the field of AI."

"AI? Artificial intelligence? How has that affected things?"

"As humans, *homo sapiens*, we've evolved over hundreds of thousands of years here on Earth, but we don't have the capacity to think globally or in extremely long-time frames. Hunter-gatherers didn't need to think like that. We're simply bad at having a big-picture mindset and acting in ways that are sustainable for future generations. The AI-based decision-support systems and future simulators that the world's governments and organizations now have access to have convincingly shown us that we were rapidly heading toward total destruction. All the independent AI systems dealing with future issues reached the same conclusion."

"Wow! That's interesting!"

"Yes! Humanity's only chance to successfully tackle the climate issue is to stop wasting human and economic resources on wars and armed conflicts and instead put all our efforts and resources into slowing down climate change."

"You said the world has suffered terrible climate disasters."

"Yes, tens, maybe hundreds of millions of people have died in climate-related disasters around the world over the past decades. It's horrifying, but it might have also been the wake-up call humanity needed."

"Wow, it's clearly a very different world now."

"Yes, and it's going to take some time to update you on how things are today. I hope we'll get the time to do that."

"I hope so too, but we'll have to take it one step at a time. Right now, I'm overwhelmed by everything you've told me so far."

"Rashid, you said you're innocent of what you've been accused of. Do you think there's a way to prove your innocence?"

"Maybe, but we can talk about that later. I also want you to explain why a deportation to the US might be considered. I don't understand why the US would want me; I don't get it at all. But right now, I mainly want to know why we're down here. What happened?"

"OK, I'll explain. I arrived here this morning via the night train from Eskilstuna to Östersund. I had booked a *hotainer* all the way to this prison, and Sara was going to meet me for breakfast in the cafeteria before I was to meet you."

"*Hotainer?* What's that?"

"You don't know? It's clear you've been out of touch with the real world for several years. A hotainer is a combination of a hotel room and a container. They come in different sizes and variations but usually have a bed, a toilet, a shower, and a small kitchenette with a fridge, freezer, and microwave. The big advantage is that you can go to sleep in one place and be quietly and smoothly transported to another, usually during the night. The transportation can happen by train, truck, or transport drone, and it can even involve switching between modes of transport. I went to bed in Eskilstuna last night and woke up well-rested here at the Grey Mountain Prison. During the trip, two transfers were made. The first one was in Stockholm, from one train to another, and the second was in Östersund, from train to road transport. I didn't notice the transfers at all. I slept soundly during the whole journey; the transport was that smooth. They use active noise and vibration cancellation, along with smart G-force compensators. Normally, you don't even notice that the hotainer has moved."

"How smart and comfortable."

"Yes, you can go to bed in one place and wake up somewhere else without realizing you've been moved. This has become an incredibly popular way to travel. You can also choose for how long you want access to the hotainer; for example, you can book it for a whole night even if the trip only takes a few hours."

"How smart and comfortable, but now I really want to know what happened to us. It's really frustrating that you're spending so much time explaining other things in detail, even though they're interesting. Why are we down here, and why might we be stuck here for a long time?"

"But you asked me what a hotainer was."

"Come on, now!"

"Okay, here's what happened. I was waiting in the reception area outside the prison cafeteria after taking a short walk around the premises, waiting for it to be 9 o'clock. Sara came in through the main door with you. You both looked very cold in your thick coats, and you Rashid were wearing large dark sunglasses even though it was a gray, cloudy October morning."

"The sunglasses, you know why I've been forced to wear them. They're just so others don't have to see how awful my face looks."

"After we greeted each other, Sara explained that you'd just taken a walk and that she had just told you that you were going to meet me."

"I don't remember meeting you."

"Even though it happened just a few hours ago?"

"No, I vaguely remember the walk with Sara, but not that we met."

"Suddenly, I saw through the windows that everything outside was lit up by an enormously bright and blinding light. Sara, who normally never swears, yelled loudly, *'Hell, what's happening'* and grabbed the edge of a wall-mounted information board right next to where we were standing. She slid the large board aside, and behind it, there was an elevator door that opened, revealing a rather cramped elevator with eight fixed seats equipped with seatbelts, four on each side. Sara pushed both you and me into the elevator and yelled at us to sit down and buckle up. I helped you into a seat, sat down across from you, and fastened my seatbelt. It was a bit tricky since we were still wearing our coats. I tried to reach across the cramped elevator to fasten your seatbelt too. Sara shouted, *'Damn, the ankle monitor, I'll be right back, I just need to get ...'* but in the middle of that sentence, the lights suddenly went out, the elevator doors slammed shut, and it felt like the elevator was plunging downwards in what I can only describe as freefall."

"Freefall straight down? How long did that fall last? Did we fall far?"

"After a few seconds, the elevator suddenly stopped, and I think you fell forward, hitting your head on the edge of my seat."

"Oh my God ... "

"I noticed with my feet that you were lying on the floor in front of me, and I could hear you groaning for a while before you went completely silent. Unfortunately, I hadn't managed to fasten your seatbelt."

"I don't remember anything of what you're telling me."

"After another second or two, I heard a metallic grinding noise, and the elevator doors opened. It was total darkness, and I couldn't see a thing. I unbuckled my seatbelt and pulled your limp body out of the elevator. After a few meters, I bumped into a steel door. I managed, after a bit of fumbling in the dark, to open the door by pulling up two 30 centimeters long handles and then, with some effort, dragging the heavy door towards me. I dragged you through the opening into the next room, closed the heavy door behind us, and pressed down the long handles on the other side of the door."

"Just in case ..."

"Where you were lying on the floor, I could feel with my hand that you were bleeding quite a lot from your forehead. I took off my jacket, sweater, and shirt, tore the shirt into strips, and tied them together to make a kind of bandage, which I wrapped around your head in the darkness to try to stop the bleeding."

"Thanks for helping me, but as I said, I don't remember any of that. It's so strange."

"It's probably a concussion causing memory loss for the event."

"That blinding light, what do you think caused it?"

"I don't know. Maybe a nuclear explosion, maybe a bright burning meteor that entered the atmosphere, maybe a crashing satellite, or something else."

"Like what?"

"Maybe an electrical surge nearby, in a power line or a transformer station. Maybe some new type of laser weapon. I don't know, I'm just wildly guessing now."

"If it was a nuclear explosion, wouldn't we have also felt a massive shockwave?"

"Yes, but light travels much faster than the shockwave, and maybe we got underground before the shockwave hit. The explosion could've been miles away."

"Didn't you hear any sound together with the blinding light?"

"Nothing that I noticed, but everything happened so fast and suddenly."

"Ugh, how scary. I wonder what happened to Sara."

"Yes, and to everyone else up there."

CHAPTER 4

"Fredrik, you've apparently already had time to explore this place while I was unconscious. I'd also like to get a sense of what's down here. Can we go through the spaces together so I can familiarize myself with what's around?"

"Of course. We can start at the steel door where I pulled you out of the elevator. Come, I'll take you there. Here, take my hand."

"You don't seem as shaky as you were earlier. Have you started getting used to the situation we're in?"

"Maybe your calmness has rubbed off on me. Now we're at the steel door. This is where I pulled you after that dramatic elevator ride when you got bloodied and lost consciousness."

"Do you think we'll be able to get out the same way?"

"I don't know, but I don't want to try just yet. It could be dangerous up there."

"In what way?"

"Maybe radiation, maybe people who mean us harm, maybe toxic conditions in some way. I don't know. It's also possible that it's completely safe up there, outside, but I want to be cautious."

"That sounds reasonable."

"I wonder what it was that triggered the evacuation elevator."

"Evacuation elevator? What kind of elevator is that?"

"Sara told me last summer about this elevator. It was originally built so people could quickly reach this underground bunker in case of an emergency situation. Back then, this was a military facility. When Grey Mountain Fortress, as it was called, was converted into a prison and renamed the Grey Mountain Prison, they renovated the elevator. They realized that there might be a need for the prison staff to quickly get to safety during a threatening situation, so the evacuation elevator retained its important function."

"How long ago did it become a prison?"

"About 20 years ago. You were one of the first prisoners to end up here."

"Was I?"

"Now, if we stand with our backs to the door, we have a corridor about 10 meters long in front of us. At the other end of the corridor, there's another typical bunker door, but it has two large hand-wheels for opening and closing instead of long levers."

"Why's that?"

"No idea."

"Please continue."

"Along the corridor, on each side, there are doors to rooms, but these doors are more like regular interior doors, not heavy bunker doors. Let's start by checking what's on the left side of the corridor. Right here, near the wall, I found a crank mounted at waist height next to a vertical metal pipe. I think the crank can be used to manually pump fresh air if needed. Feel the pipe here!"

"Fredrik, should we start cranking? Want me to get it going?"

"No, I don't think that's necessary. The air feels pretty good down here, don't you think?"

"It feels fine."

"As we continue down the left side, here's a door that leads to a room with a few shelves covered in waxed cloth or something like plastic material, but the shelves are empty. Come in with me ... "

"You're right, I can't feel anything on the shelves either, but what's that smell in here?"

"It smells a little like my grandmother's pantry."

"That's probably right. I've never been in your grandmother's pantry, but I can smell a faint scent of food. This room might've been a food storage area. Now I'm starting to feel a little hungry. Have you found any food down here?"

"Unfortunately not."

"Oh no, we might be in trouble then. What's this big metal container in the back of the room? Is it a water tank?"

"I think so, but if you knock on it, it sounds empty. At the bottom, there's a faucet, and when I tried turning it earlier, nothing came out. Speaking of water and food, let's move on to the next room."

"Okay."

"This is a slightly larger room that you've already been in. This is where we sat down at the table earlier when I was trying to explain why we're down here. It's probably a break room, dining room, or meeting room, maybe a combination. There are eight chairs around the table."

"Plenty of room for the two of us, then."

"Come, over here is a small kitchenette. Feel this, there's a hot plate, a microwave, and a little sink with a faucet, the same kind as the one in the restroom. I've tested the faucet, and just like in the restroom, only cold water comes out."

"Have you tasted the water?"

"Yes. The water smelled okay after I let it run for a bit. I've also tasted it, and it didn't taste bad. It's probably the same water that comes from the restroom sink. It was cold and felt almost a bit fresh. I think the water is fine. My stomach hasn't complained yet, but if there's something wrong with the water, it might take a while before we notice."

"Well, at least we won't die of thirst."

"A small comfort in our situation."

"Have you tried to see if the hot plate or microwave works?"

"Both are completely dead, probably because we don't have any electric power."

"Oh, so we'll only be eating cold food ... if we had any."

"Was that meant as a joke?"

"Humor can help you cope with almost anything. I once read a really interesting book, I think it was called *Laugh or Cry,* where it talked about how many of the Jews in concentration camps during World War II joked a lot, and often quite darkly, about their hopeless situation. They joked even though they were fully aware of what was likely awaiting them. It was a way to keep control of something, and maybe it also worked as a silent protest against the oppressors, they wouldn't control everything."

"I think I understand. Go ahead and joke if you think it'll help us."

"Maybe I will. We'll see ... said the blind man."

"Here we have a fridge, but it's empty and, of course, completely dead. The kitchen cabinets above the sink are also almost completely empty. The only things I found were four mugs and four soup bowls. No food!"

"Well, at least we can eat two meals without washing dishes ... if we had any food. Have you found any other kitchen equipment?"

"In a drawer under the counter where the hot plate is, I found four forks, four knives, and four spoons, along with a can opener and a corkscrew."

"The corkscrew will be handy when we need to celebrate something."

"Mmm ... "

"No frying pans or pots?"

"No, the lower cabinets were completely empty."

"It seems like we'll have to rely on takeout. Fredrik, should we order a couple of pizzas to be delivered down here?"

"Rashid, are you really that hungry? You seem completely fixated on food."

"You think? Let's try not to think about food right now. It'll just make things worse."

"But you were the one who just brought up pizza."

"Sorry."

"Over here on the long wall, there's a large whiteboard, and on the shelf or ledge below the board are two pens that smell like alcohol when you take the caps off."

"What colors are the pens?"

"Hello, do you think I've been lying when I said it's totally dark down here?"

"If the pens work, we could write our goodbye notes on the board."

"Rashid, you're so positive."

"I've got only one problem."

"What's that?"

"I don't have anyone to write a goodbye note to. Marie's dead, my parents are dead, and I don't even know if my little sister Samira is alive."

"What happened to your little sister?"

"She was kidnapped when she was seven years old."

"That's terrible. How did it happen?"

"Can we talk about it later? I don't want to discuss it right now. Those memories are hard to talk about."

"Absolutely. I understand."

"What about you? Do you have a family? A wife, partner, any kids?"

"No, unfortunately not."

"Parents?"

"Both my parents died just a few years ago. They drowned in New York."

"I'm sorry to hear that, but how do you drown in New York? What happened?"

"The levees and walls that had been built to prevent flooding weren't high enough or strong enough. A combination of high tide, a long period of extreme rainfall, and a hurricane that surpassed all previous ones in strength was just too much. The barriers broke at Battery Park on the southern tip of Manhattan. For a couple of years, there had been repeated flood warnings for New York due to extreme weather, but nothing serious had happened. This lulled the city's residents into a false sense of security, and when another warning came, many ignored the danger, including those responsible for ordering the evacuation of the subway system when the risk of flooding was imminent. The consequences were devastating. Over 8,000 people died, most of them in the subway. That's where my parents were when the water flooded in."

"Were they on vacation in New York?"

"No, both my parents worked for the UN at the time and were in New York to prepare for the relocation of the UN headquarters from New York to Jerusalem."

"To Jerusalem? How in the world ... Why would they do that?"

"It was a way to try to solve the almost eternal conflict over the city that still means so much to different religions. Since several religions see Jerusalem as their religious center and since both Israelis and Palestinians have claimed the city, the UN decided to make Jerusalem and its surrounding areas international territory and to move its headquarters there. They had been discussing and even trying both a one-state solution and a two-state solution for decades. In the end, it became an *all-state solution* under UN protection. That way, Jerusalem became owned, governed, and protected by all of us, by all the world's countries, through the UN."

"Interesting, but what a tragedy for your parents. Do you have any siblings?"

"No, not anymore. I also had a little sister, but she died of an overdose when she was just 14 years old."

"Oh my God, that's terrible. Was she using drugs even though she was so young?"

"Not that we knew of in the family. It came suddenly and shocked us all. We think it might have been the first time she tried it. It was some kind of new synthetic drug, and it happened at one of her friend's houses. The friend was saved at the last minute and said afterward that she and my sister just wanted to try it out. We never found out where they got the pills."

"What a shock that must have been for your family."

"It's the worst thing I've ever experienced."

"Fredrik, do you have a girlfriend or anything?"

"That's a matter of definition."

"What do you mean?"

"I interact virtually with a woman who lives on Hawaii's biggest island, Big Island, but we've never met. I hope I'll get to visit her someday, but we'll see how that goes now. Her name is Dolores, and she's a researcher studying exoplanets."

"Fascinating. I hope you get to meet her in person someday."

"I hope so too. Come on, let's check the next room."

"I'm coming."

"You've been here before. This is the restroom, so we can skip that now."

"Right, but what were those barrels in the corner?"

"They're probably reserve toilets in case the other one doesn't work. The barrels are stacked three by three and have both seats and lids. I think they're called dry toilets."

"Okay, you have a lot to say about these barrels. I give a shit."

"That's exactly what I think we shouldn't do, at least not as long as the regular toilet is functioning."

"I get it, I was just ... "

"Here's the last room on the left side, a small cleaning closet. In here, there's a broom, a dustpan, a bucket, a mop, a plastic bottle that I guess contains some soap or something similar, and there's also a vacuum cleaner."

"Have you tried to see if it works?"

"No, but since we don't have any lights, no working microwave, and a dead fridge, I don't think it's worth trying. Besides, I don't feel like starting to vacuum right now."

"You haven't found an electrical panel or a main switch for the electricity?"

"I've looked but haven't found one."

"When I felt along the walls in the rooms we've been in, I didn't find one either. The electrical wiring runs along the walls but doesn't seem to lead to any power panel in the rooms we have access to."

"Okay, Rashid, now we're at the other steel door, the one with the hand-wheels."

"What do you think is on the other side of this door?"

"I don't know, but I wonder if it has a connection to the old weapons factory, meaning the prison where your cell is and where you've spent many years."

"What? Has the Grey Mountain Prison been a weapons factory before? I didn't know that even though I've been here so long."

"There's a lot you don't know when you choose to shut yourself off from all contact with other people. Yes, this place was once a huge underground weapons factory. I think I read somewhere that it was more than 10,000 square-meters in size and that around a hundred people worked there."

"Where we are now, was this also part of the large weapons factory?"

"Where we are now was probably a separate unit, and what Sara told me indicates that it might have been an extra confidential and sensitive operation right here."

"How do you know?"

"When she asked the person in charge of renovating the elevator what had previously been here, the response she got was a little odd. The person said it was a part of Sweden's history that probably should just be erased and forgotten. When Sara tried to ask more, she didn't get an answer."

"Do you have any idea what it could have been?"

"No, but I guess it involved some type of weapon development because it was next to the large weapons factory, but I don't know for sure."

"What kind of weapons could they have been working on?"

"Maybe they were dealing with the development of chemical or biological weapons, or some other type of controversial weapons."

"What did they manufacture in the large underground factory, and when was that factory operational?"

"I think it was sometime in the 1940s, and it was mainly bombs for the air force that they made here. There was an air base in Östersund, not too far from here."

"And when did they convert the underground space into a prison?"

"That was about 20 years ago. I think I mentioned it earlier."

"Why did they convert an old weapons factory into a prison?"

"There was a massive need for new prison spaces. Old underground facilities became an option. The advantage with these is that they can be made very escape-proof, making underground prisons especially suitable for the most dangerous criminals. This underground prison is also for some reason a rather secret facility. Very few people know about its existence."

"So, I was apparently considered one of Sweden's most dangerous criminals?"

"Yes, Rashid, that's right, you were considered, and are still considered, one of the most dangerous. That's why you've been kept here in this prison."

"But why would I be seen as so extremely dangerous?"

"Now let's turn around and see what's on the other side of the corridor. Welcome in, here we have a small dormitory with two bunk beds and four metal lockers. It's a small room for four people, each with their own locker. The beds have some sort of springy metal frame, but there are no mattresses or bed linens here."

"Are we going to be forced to sleep in those beds if we have to stay here for a while? It doesn't seem very comfortable."

"Maybe so, we don't have many other options, but come with me to the next room."

"I'm coming."

"Here's another dormitory, identical to the other one. Again, there are two bunk beds without mattresses and four lockers."

"Hooray, we can each have our own bedroom."

"Good if one of us snores. You can also choose freely if you want the upper or lower bunk."

"What I'd really like is a mattress, a pillow, and a blanket."

"Let's move on to the next room. Come on!"

"Okay, I'm coming!"

"This is a fairly large room with a number of metal shelves. There are quite a few cardboard boxes on the shelves, and it seems like there's something in these boxes. That's what it felt like when I lifted a few of the boxes. This room appears to be some sort of storage area."

"I hope it's food in the boxes. Haven't you checked?"

"No, I haven't."

"Why not?"

"I didn't have time when I was checking the rooms earlier. I also had to keep an eye on you and make sure you were okay. In the beginning, I was also afraid I would get lost. I had no idea how big or small it was down here. When I was half-panicked, rushing around in the dark, I bumped into furniture, shelves, door frames, and other things. I also stumbled badly a few times. I probably have lots of bruises."

"It was kind of you to keep an eye on me. Should we check what's in the boxes now? I hope it's something edible."

"We can do that."

"In this box, there are things wrapped in bubble wrap. I'll open one and try to feel what it is with my hands."

"What is it?"

"Fredrik, this seems like something really weird. It feels like a small figure, maybe a little troll with a fuzzy hairstyle. Why on earth do they have a storage of these figures down here?"

"I think I know. They're troll figures. Sara told me that a few years ago, the prison had a warden who had a bunch of creative, but sometimes strange, ideas about how to keep the inmates busy. One of his ideas was for the prisoners to make *Jämtland Trolls'* and sell them to tourists. He wanted to design them himself, but his artistic skills were apparently not great. The trolls' appearance was a disaster according to Sara, and they were apparently so hideously ugly and scary that they couldn't be sold. The trolls were made of concrete and had hair made of sheep's wool. The staff wanted the troll inventory to be thrown away, but the warden refused, so they apparently ended up here in this storage room."

"Fredrik, at least there's a lot of bubble wrap around the trolls. Maybe we can use that to make beds in the bunks."

"Just as long as you don't pop the bubble wrap all night. That sound can be pretty annoying."

"Yeah, but you'll have your own room."

"It seems like there are two full shelves of troll boxes. I think we have 32 boxes of trolls. There are probably eight trolls in each box. What does that make? It must be 256."

"So we have 256 trolls, 256 reportedly hideous concrete trolls that are also inedible. Ugh!"

"But hey, there are more shelves with boxes of a completely different size. Maybe we'll find something better."

"What? Concrete Santa figures?"

"You're so positive."

"As always!"

"Now, Rashid! Maybe this will cheer you up. In this box, there are a bunch of tin cans that feel like canned food. Yep, they really feel like cans. The cans have rings you can pull to open them. Should I open one?"

"Of course! Do it! I can open one too."

"Wait! Maybe we should hold off on opening them until we've thought it through. What if there's a risk? What if it's some kind of weapon? Could there be old chemical agents in the cans?"

"Coward."

"But maybe there's no risk since they have pull rings. Wait! I think I've figured out what's in the cans."

"What? How can you know?"

"Sara told me that the warden with the troll idea also thought that the inmates could work as foster carers for the dogs used by the police, the military, and customs. He thought the prisoners would be calmed by working with animals and that they could do something meaningful. They started on a small scale, and it worked really well until someone reported that the dogs were spending too much time underground without natural sunlight. It became a question of animal welfare, and the program was shut down, but the warden had already ordered a ton of dog food, probably including these canned dog foods we've got here in our underground storage."

"I wonder what the expiration date is on these cans."

"I guess that's something we'll keep wondering about."

"So we're going to eat dog food ... and only dog food ... for the foreseeable future. And with our limited cooking facilities, it'll always be cold dog food. I'm suddenly not as hungry anymore."

"If the alternative is to starve to death, maybe dog food isn't so bad. I've also read somewhere that dog food is actually safe for humans to eat. Maybe not delicious, but perfectly edible."

"Should we wait to open the remaining boxes, which probably just contain trolls and dog food, and instead check out the next room?"

"We can, but you're going to be surprised."

"Why? Now you've got me really curious. Is there real food there?"

"Unfortunately not. Come and see what's behind the next door. Feel here, beyond the door, the entrance is completely bricked up. You can feel the large masonry blocks or concrete blocks they used; the mortar seams are very noticeable. You can probably guess what's behind it. It's likely the old weapons development lab that's been sealed off."

"I definitely don't want to go in there."

"You can't, either."

"Good!"

"Rashid, we've completed the tour. What do you think we should do now?"

"I don't know. What do you think?"

"I think we should go back to the storage room, empty some of the boxes, and take those and some bubble wrap to the dorm rooms and make beds as best we can. Empty boxes will be our mattresses, and bubble wrap will be our blankets. Then we can lie down for a while, rest, and think about what to do next."

"Okay, but I'm actually getting a little hungry."

"Are you ready to try the canned contents now?"

"No, not quite yet. Let's go and make the beds like you suggested."

"Shouldn't we each have our own bedroom? I think we should."

"Absolutely, I agree."

"Which room do you want?"

"It doesn't matter. I'll take the one closest to the door with the hand-wheels."

"Then I'll take the other one."

"Did you remember to bring your pajamas and toothbrush?"

"Rashid, you're hopeless."

CHAPTER 5

"Fredrik, can you hear me if I talk to you from the room next door?"

"Yeah, no problem, as long as we keep the doors open. But if you start snoring, I'll shut them."

"Have you made your bed yet?"

"Yeah, and it's not too bad with boxes and bubble wrap, but I'm still wearing my outer clothes. It makes it warmer and softer."

"I'm still in my outer clothes too. Did you take the top or bottom bunk?"

"I chose the top bunk, though I'm not sure why I made that choice. Maybe because I've never slept in the top bunk of a bunk bed before."

"I took the bottom one simply because it's easier to get in and out of."

"Have you thought about the air down here, the air we breathe?"

"No, what do you mean? I think it's fine. The only thing I've noticed is the whooshing sound from the vents; there's one right above the door in here. It's the same faint whooshing sound as in my cell. The ventilation sounds exactly the same."

"That's exactly what I mean. We don't seem to have any electricity down here, but we still seem to have a functioning supply of fresh air. I wonder how that works. What's powering the ventilation fans? Is it regular outdoor air being pumped down here? If the air up there gets dangerous, do we run the risk of breathing it down here? Or is this a bomb shelter-type ventilation system with filters that remove harmful substances? Could it be a simple ventilation system installed when the prison part was built?"

"Great, another thing to worry about. But breathe we must, or we'll die."

"Do you want me to shut up now so you can sleep?"

"You know, I won't be able to sleep for a while. Too many thoughts are spinning around in my head."

"Same here. What are you thinking about the most ... besides food?"

"That I'm considered one of Sweden's most dangerous prisoners and that I'm at risk of deportation to the US. I really don't understand why. Can you explain that to me?"

"Do you really not understand?"

"I know I've been accused and probably convicted in Iran for the murder of my employer at the brick factory, but that doesn't make me one of Sweden's most dangerous prisoners. Plus, I'm innocent."

"But what about the attack in Norway?"

"What attack?"

"The one where 28 NATO soldiers were killed, most of them from the US."

"What? What are you talking about?"

"Outside Trondheim. Your explosive charge caused a landslide that dragged the bus into the fjord, drowning everyone, and it was your phone that triggered the explosion."

"My God, what are these fantasies? How could I have done that? I've never even been to Norway, not once."

"The investigators concluded that it was your phone that was used to trigger the explosion. There are also surveillance videos of you with the backpack. You were caught on film at the gas station where you parked the car."

"But I've never been to Norway. Never, ever!"

"When the helicopter shot you outside Ånge, they had tracked your phone, the same phone you used to trigger the explosion. And you were wearing the same backpack as the one in the surveillance footage from the gas station in Norway. They also found traces of a specific explosive in the backpack, the same type of explosive that was used to trigger the landslide. I've read the investigation report. The evidence is compelling."

"But, but … "

"How can you claim you weren't involved?"

"My God, I think I get it now. I should never have picked up that damn backpack! That's why they shot me! My God!"

"What do you mean? What are you talking about?"

"The day I was shot, the day Marie was killed, I was standing under a bridge near my hiding place, fishing. Normally, I use a simple bamboo fishing pole when I fish under the bridge, but this time I used spin fishing gear because I had planned to fish with a spinning rod at a pond a bit further away. On the way to the pond, near the bridge, Marie noticed there were a lot of blueberries growing, so she wanted to stop for a while to pick some. I think fishing is more fun than picking berries, so I took my spinning rod and went down under the bridge while Marie busied herself with her blueberry picking. I stood on a ledge close to one of the bridge's supports, right under the bridge, to stay out of sight in case anyone drove over it. That road had very little traffic, mostly just a few timber trucks and sometimes service vehicles heading to or from the wind farm."

"Go on … "

"But that day, something unusual happened. I heard a car speeding up, then screeching to a halt on the bridge. A car door opened, and a second later, there was a loud splash in the water just a few meters in front of me."

"What did they throw down?"

"It sank so quickly to the bottom that I didn't see what it was. After a few seconds, I heard the car door shut. The car turned around, sped off quickly, and headed back in the direction it had come from. Since I had seen exactly where the thing had landed, I instinctively cast my fishing lure, an inline spinner, beyond that spot, let it sink to the bottom, and reeled it in. I repeated this a few times, and on the third attempt, I hooked something. It was really heavy, and I was afraid my line would snap. Eventually, I managed to pull it close enough to see that it was a backpack. I grabbed it with my hands and dragged it onto the ledge where I was standing. When I opened the backpack, I saw that it contained a few fist-sized rocks, but there was also a rolled-up jacket, a knitted hat, and a pair of gloves. I took out the rocks and examined the jacket. In an inner pocket, there was an iPhone that, to my surprise, was still on and seemed to have survived its short time in the water. Why had someone thrown a backpack with a jacket and an iPhone into the water? I realized that the rocks were meant to sink the backpack, and the whole thing seemed very suspicious."

"Yeah, why did they do that?"

"My first instinct was to turn the backpack and its contents over to the police, but I immediately realized that I couldn't do that since I was a wanted man. I needed to consult Marie, so I hid my fishing gear on top of one of the bridge supports and started walking briskly toward where Marie was picking blueberries. I had slung the wet backpack over my shoulders, on top of my waterproof fishing jacket."

"What did Marie say?"

"She didn't have time to say anything. After I had walked a couple hundred meters, all hell broke loose."

"How so? What happened?"

"The first thing that hit me was the noise. It came so fast and suddenly. A helicopter flew in at an extremely low altitude, treetop level, directly toward me, and it started firing immediately. I felt a sharp pain in my right leg, and I fell. As I lay on the ground, I saw Marie running toward me, a bit further up the slope, and behind her was a timber truck. She must not have seen or heard the truck because of the helicopter, because suddenly she stepped out onto the road, and ... and ... "

"I know. It must have been awful."

"Her head was crushed by the truck's front wheel, and I knew instantly that her life was over. At that moment, it also felt like my life ended. Seeing Marie's head crushed was the last thing my eyes ever saw and the last thing I can remember from that day. That image will never leave me. But thank God I also have other images of Marie ... beautiful memories of her."

"How incredibly horrible that must have been ... "

"Fredrik, it's strange. I don't remember what happened to you and me this morning, with the elevator and all that ... but that event by the bridge ... even though it was so many years ago, it feels like I remember every single second."

"Rashid, are you okay? Do you want me to come into your room?"

"No, please stay in your room. I really want to be alone for a while … "

"Let me know if you change your mind. Do you want us to stop talking about that incident?"

"What more is there to say?"

"According to what I read in the criminal investigation report; you were shot a second time from the helicopter while you were lying on the ground. This time, you were hit by several bullets, some of which struck your head. That's when both of your eyes were so severely damaged that you lost your sight completely, and you also suffered injuries to the left side of your brain. It was these injuries that were later thought to have caused a severe form of aphasia. The shots to your head were fired around the same time Marie was killed by the truck. They used a small-caliber weapon from the helicopter, and the intention wasn't to kill you. On the contrary, the report states that the mission was to incapacitate you. They specifically used that word in the investigation report: *incapacitate*. They didn't want you dead. They wanted to interrogate you to try to get more information about the attack in Norway."

"So they shot me several times in the head from a helicopter, with no intention of killing me. That sounds strange and not very convincing."

"The report says it was a mistake that you were shot in the head and injured so severely. Marie's death is also described as a pure accident. During questioning, the driver of the timber truck said he had been watching the helicopter and didn't see the woman running along the road."

"What else did the report say?"

"There were quite a few unanswered questions. For example, what happened to the car they tried to follow? Despite extensive efforts, they never found it. They also couldn't track down or identify the other people suspected of being involved in the attack in Norway. Besides you, there were at least three other people involved. That was determined by studying surveillance footage and compiling all the witness reports."

"Fredrik, so you still believe that I was involved in that attack?"

"No, of course not. After what you just told me, I'm convinced you're innocent."

"Thank you!"

"I was only trying to recount what the investigation concluded. The motive for the attack was also something that was discussed. In your case, they assumed that, since you're from Afghanistan, the US's involvement in the war there might explain your participation."

"My supposed participation ... "

"Yes, ... sorry. The soaking wet backpack also puzzled the investigators, and one possible explanation was that you might have accidentally dropped it into some water, while another theory was that you had tried to sink it but then changed your mind. They found traces of bottom sediment in the fabric."

"If only they had known the full truth about what really happened. Then my situation would now be completely different."

"Yes, then you probably wouldn't have had to spend all these years in prison, and Marie might still be alive today."

"If only I hadn't fished up that backpack. That was obviously a big mistake."

"Coincidences and chance can have enormous consequences. What if your girlfriend hadn't been so fond of blueberries? Then maybe you would have been at the pond fishing when the backpack was dumped from the bridge. That would have changed everything."

"So you're saying it's all Marie's fault, is that really what you are saying?"

"No, but you shouldn't blame yourself either. That is totally wrong."

"But I'm allowed to be disappointed and angry that the investigators drew completely wrong conclusions. It's a heavy feeling to know that my and Marie's lives were destroyed because of other people's mistakes. The whole thing feels downright awful."

"Today, criminal investigations are of much better quality. Since AI was introduced, there are far fewer mistakes. With AI support, huge amounts of information can be analyzed and interpreted in a very short time, and the systems can identify and use historical parallels to what happened. In the past, it was easy for investigators to emotionally or subconsciously get stuck on a particular lead. AI systems usually don't make such mistakes. They impartially evaluate all possible alternatives in criminal investigations."

"You say AI systems are more impartial than humans. Is that really the case? Don't they ever draw the wrong conclusions?"

"Of course they can. That's why at least three completely independent and certified AI systems are used to process the same information for each case, and then the outcomes are compared."

"That sounds like a reasonable setup. What does it mean when you say the AI systems are *certified?*"

"Certified AI systems have been checked and approved by the National Verification Agency. There's no doubt that legal certainty has improved since investigators and lawyers started using AI support."

CHAPTER 6

"Rashid, are you awake?"

"Now I am, but I think I did sleep for a little while. I do think I dozed off a bit."

"I know you were sleeping. Your snoring was pretty loud."

"How long did I sleep?"

"No idea. I've slept for a while too. But without a clock and no working ComU, I have no clue how long you or I have been asleep or what time it is."

"My feeling, but it's just a guess, is that I dozed off for a few hours."

"Rashid, when you were telling me about the incident at the bridge, you said it was near your hideout. Can you tell me more about that hideout? Was that where you stayed because of the deportation order?"

"That's right. The hideout I mentioned was a summer cabin, a cabin that belonged to Marie's aunt."

"A summer cabin? Did you both live there, you and Marie? "

"Not both of us, just me. Marie was only there sometimes. She called it a summer cabin even though it was perfectly fine to stay there in winter too."

"I see …"

"When I got the deportation order to Iran, I panicked and told Marie that it was basically a death sentence for me. Marie thought I should go into hiding until we could figure out a way to get the decision overturned. She told me she had an aunt, Elsa, who owned the place, but it wasn't being used because Elsa had been placed in a dementia care home. After Marie's parents died in a car accident in Tenerife when she was only 18, her aunt and her aunt's husband, Erik, became like surrogate parents to her."

"Did Marie's parents also live in Ånge?"

"No, they lived in Arboga, where both worked as high school teachers. That's also where Marie was born and raised, but she didn't talk much about her parents or her childhood there. I don't know why, maybe that was her way of dealing with the grief. Her aunt had also told Marie that one day she would inherit the summer cabin. Elsa and Erik didn't have any children, and Marie didn't have any siblings. Marie also had permission to use the cabin whenever she wanted, as much as she liked. She even had her own set of keys. The property originally belonged to Marie's grandparents, who lived there year-round. Back then, it was a small homestead with a piece of farmland and a small patch of forest. They lived off farming, forestry, and some fishing. Since the place was very secluded, a bit outside the main town, Marie thought it would be the perfect hiding spot for me."

"And the main town was Ånge, right?"

"Yes, that's where the shops and other services were. The property also had a unique advantage. The electricity was free, so thanks to the cabin's electric heating, I could live there quite discreetly, even in the winter, without anyone seeing smoke coming from the chimney."

"How was the electricity free?"

"When the local power company built the large hydro power dam, much of the farm's land ended up underwater, and as partial compensation, the property was granted free electricity for as long as the power plant generates electricity. Just a few days after the deportation order, I moved to the cabin from the refugee center outside Uppsala. Marie, who was studying to become a medical doctor, paused her studies, and after just a few weeks, she moved to Ånge, where she rented a small apartment near the center. She quickly found a job in home care, which was perfect because part of the job involved driving around the municipality to help elderly people who still lived in their homes. That way, she could sometimes bring me some food and other supplies when she was nearby. The home care schedules were very tight, so often the visits were very short, but when she had a day off from work, she stayed a bit longer. To minimize the risk of anyone discovering I was hiding there, we tried not to see each other too often."

"So she gave up her medical studies to help you."

"Marie put it differently. She said she was just pausing her studies and that working in home care gave her valuable practical experience that would be very useful in her future career as a medical doctor. Her intention was to resume her studies later."

"Sounds like she was a very kind and caring person."

"Yes, she was absolutely amazing. I've never met a more loving person."

"How did you two meet?"

"She and I happened to sit next to each other on a grassy slope while we were both watching the students river rafting event at the Walpurgis Night celebrations in Uppsala. For some reason, we started talking. After sitting there for a while and talking about all sorts of things, she invited me over for coffee at the student dorm where she lived. Then things just kept going from there, and we actually became a couple after just a few weeks. But we did everything we could to keep our relationship secret. In case the Migration Board decided to deport me, we didn't want the authorities, especially the police, to be able to see any connection between me and Marie. That would make it harder for her to help me stay hidden."

"How long did you stay hidden in the cabin?"

"When I got shot and Marie was killed, I had been hiding there for about two years."

"What did you do during the days?"

"Marie wanted me to learn to speak Swedish well as soon as possible. She believed that it would make it much easier for me to stay in Sweden. She made sure that I was almost constantly *immersed* in the Swedish language."

"*Immersed* in the Swedish language?"

"Yes, by that she meant that I should hear and actively use Swedish as much as possible. She wanted me to only listen to Swedish programs on the radio, preferably just the talk channel P1, and to only watch Swedish programs on TV. There were also tons of videotapes and DVDs with Swedish movies in the summer cabin, plus a lot of Swedish audiobooks on CD and DVD."

"Did Marie arrange all that? She must have been very driven."

"The movies, CDs and DVDs were already there."

"Why?"

"Erik, Aunt Elsa's husband, loved watching movies and listening to books. He worked for a local trucking company where he drove a timber truck and sometimes a mail truck to various places in the northern part of Sweden. In the truck's cab, he always listened to audiobooks, and he amassed a large collection. When others started listening to books and watching movies online, he received a bunch of books and movies on CD and DVD from friends and colleagues. He was a bit of a hoarder when it came to audiobooks and films. Everything was in Swedish because he hadn't learned English or any other foreign language."

"Apparently, he didn't need any other languages."

"No, that's right. He also made sure to have several sets of VCRs and other playback devices that could handle video tapes and both CDs and DVDs. He wanted to be sure he could watch movies and listen to books even when the equipment for it was no longer available in stores. In the cabin's attic, there were many VCRs, DVD players, and TVs. If any device broke, he wanted to have spares. Marie said he was a huge book and movie lover. Erik had said that when he retired, he would spend most of his time listening to books and watching movies."

"Did that happen?"

"No, unfortunately, he died of a heart attack the year before he was planning to retire."

"So tragic."

"Yes, very."

"What did Elsa do? What did she work with?"

"She worked as a librarian in Ånge. That's how Elsa and Erik met. At first it was the love of books that often brought Erik to the library, but later it was probably Elsa who was the main attraction. Elsa also helped expand Erik's collection of audiobooks, especially when the library switched to online audiobooks and stopped using physical media."

"Did you have internet in the cabin?"

"No, we deliberately chose not to use the internet or even cell phones. We thought it would increase the risk of being discovered. Maybe we were being overly cautious, but that's how we did it anyway."

"You never know … "

"So when I wasn't sleeping, eating, or fishing, I spent almost every waking hour watching Swedish movies and listening to Swedish books. When the radio was on, it was only the talk channel P1 that I listened to. That channel is also very educational, but for some reason, I didn't watch TV as much as I listened to the radio, except at the beginning when I watched a lot of Swedish children's programs. I think that was really good for my early language development. I did as Marie had told me, I really immersed myself in the Swedish language, almost 24/7 for two years."

"So that's why you're so damn good at Swedish. You handle the language better than many who were born here. You also seem to have a very rich vocabulary. I'm really impressed."

"It's mostly thanks to Marie."

"Rashid, let me give you an example of how language training can be done today. In Eskilstuna, I live next to a guy named Akhil, and he's just started learning Swedish. He's from Kerala in southern India and speaks three languages: English, Hindi, and Malayalam."

"But now he wants to improve his Swedish?"

"He's a climate researcher attached to Mälardalen University and has lived in Sweden for just over a year. So far, he's managed fine without knowing any Swedish since all the research and teaching is done in English. Now he's met a Swedish girl and wants to quickly learn Swedish so he can communicate better with her relatives and friends. His girlfriend helps with his language training, but what he finds most effective is the chatbot *Tutlang*, which he can access 24/7. This AI-based private tutor tailors the language training to Akhil's needs, interests, previous language knowledge, progress, and so on. Tutlang also listens carefully to how Akhil pronounces the Swedish words and how he expresses himself linguistically, correcting him in a way that's pedagogically optimal for him."

"That must be the perfect tool for learning a new language."

"Yes, it's incredibly effective, and there are similar chatbots for all kinds of subjects you want to dive into. Everyone gets the education they want, when they need it, and in a way that's best suited to that individual's interests and circumstances."

CHAPTER 7

"Rashid, I still don't understand how you can speak so easily with me ... and in Swedish, no less, which isn't your native language. Your vocabulary is so rich, and your Swedish pronunciation is fantastic."

"Thanks."

"It was only for a couple of years after you came to Sweden that you were able to live somewhat normally in society and interact with Swedish-speaking people, right?"

"I wouldn't call living in a refugee center *normal life*."

"That might have been the wrong way to put it, but you did get Swedish lessons, and you could watch Swedish TV and listen to Swedish radio… right? You were also allowed out in society."

"Yes, and I met a lot of Swedes in Uppsala, and I even made a few friends who helped me practice the language."

"Good, but after the deportation order, things changed, didn't they? You couldn't practice Swedish in the same way anymore. You were living in isolation at your hideout."

"Not entirely isolated. I had Marie ... and the books ... and the movies."

"But here in this prison, you've chosen to live in linguistic and social isolation. It's been quite a few years now ... a couple of decades. How on earth have you managed to keep your Swedish alive? You'd think you would have lost the language, and your vocal cords would have atrophied and lost their function long ago."

"In my fantasy world, I've lived a very linguistically active life. In my imagination, I've communicated with my wife Marie, my children, my friends, my coworkers, and so on. In my head, I've really kept the Swedish language alive. I've even written letters and given speeches. You wouldn't have guessed that, huh?"

"But spoken language also requires mouth movements, clearing your throat, and moistening your lips."

"I've practiced with meaningless chants and grunting to keep my vocal cords working. I once heard a guard tell his colleague that I must be really crazy because I so often speak in tongues. To be completely honest, I actually took some pleasure in playing that constant theater."

"That fantasy world of yours sounds very rich and interesting. Can you tell me more about it?"

"For now, I'd rather not. It's very private to me, and it will probably stay that way."

"Okay, I understand. I have to respect that. Is there a chance it might become a book or a movie someday?"

"Maybe, we'll see ... if we get out of here ... and if I get to live a somewhat normal life again, maybe ... but I really doubt it ... "

"I've been thinking about the questions you had about my ComU and how you used the word *cell phone*. Since you haven't communicated with people for all these years, does that mean that you haven't kept up with what's happening in the world, technologically, politically, environmentally, or in any other way?"

"I've deliberately stayed uninformed. I thought it would make it easier for me to continue with my crazy act. In the beginning, they set up a TV in my cell, but I smashed it right away. A TV set for a blind man is a bit provocative! Then they installed a speaker in the ceiling that sometimes played music and various radio programs without me being able to control what came out of the speaker. I went mad, or maybe I should say I acted mad, and pretty soon, I managed to silence the speaker by soaking a towel in water and flicking it at the speaker until it shorted out. Eventually, it died, or they turned it off. As long as the speaker was running, I would scream and shout without using real words. It was pretty hard to avoid forming actual words, but I managed to get the staff to realize that I didn't want to hear either speech or music. "

"So finally they understood."

"Yes! They didn't even try giving me newspapers or books."

"Why not?"

"Think about it. Fredrik, by now you should understand that."

"I forgot, sorry. I still don't really get why you chose total isolation."

"Partly because I hoped they wouldn't deport a blind and supposedly insane person to another country, and partly because I wanted to live undisturbed in my own fantasy world, the one I built up in my mind."

"Weren't you afraid of losing the ability to speak and the language when you didn't communicate with anyone and weren't exposed to other people talking?"

"Yes, I did worry about that, but as I said before, I used the language very intensely in my fantasy world. Often, I would also speak quietly to myself when I was fairly certain no one was listening. Sara is probably the only one who caught me once."

"How? What happened?"

"One day, when she came to my cell, she brought a little dog, it must have been a puppy. She handed the puppy to me without saying a word, and I took it. I was incredibly surprised by what she did, but despite that, I managed to stay completely silent. I heard from Sara's footsteps that she backed up a few steps, and then I heard her close the door. That made me think she had left the cell, so I started whispering to the dog while it licked my face. I think I said, *'nice dog, good dog, calm down'*, or something like that. Then I heard Sara clear her throat, like to signal that she was still in the room."

"Oh, wow!"

"She asked if I wanted to talk, and I shook my head. She said, *'I understand, and I won't say anything to the others'*. There were never any conversations between us after that, but after that incident, I thought it was totally fine when she said *'come'* or *'it's time'* when she took me for walks or *'here you go'* when she brought my food tray. But she never said anything to me if there were other people around."

"Speaking of food, how do meals work here? Do you eat with the other inmates?"

"No, I get all my meals delivered on a tray, and I eat alone in my cell. Damn, now I'm starting to feel a little hungry, talking about food."

CHAPTER 8

"Fredrik, today we're having a feast."

"What's gotten into you? Have you lost your mind?"

"I've decided to try some of that dog food or whatever's in those cans. The hunger is getting hard to bear. I figure if I drink plenty of water and just take a little bit of it, I'll soon know whether it's suitable or not. My stomach will tell me."

"Should we both try it, or is it better if just one of us goes first, and we wait for the results?"

"You mean like a ruler letting an insignificant servant or slave test the food to see if it's poisoned?"

"Rashid, do you want to be the ruler or the slave?"

"Since I suggested the whole thing, I should be the one to start. I've already grabbed a can. Come on, let's go to the kitchen. I think we should each have our own set of plates, cups, and cutlery and keep them in separate cabinets. That way, we can avoid blaming each other if someone slacks off on doing the dishes."

"Good idea. I'll take the cabinet on the far left. Did you bring two cans?"

"No, but since I'm the one trying it first, one can is more than enough. There, I've sorted everything out with my own cabinet now too. I moved all my stuff to the top cabinet on the far right."

"What should I do if you get deathly ill and can't take care of yourself?"

"That's up to you, call an ambulance, however that would work, let me die here, or try to get out and find help. Are you brave enough to leave when you don't know what's out there?"

"I'm not sure, we'll see what I do, but now I'm starting to wonder how your flesh would taste?"

"That's almost crossing the line. That was a pretty raw joke."

"A raw joke about raw meat."

"Knock it off! Now I've poured two mugs of water. I'm ready. Now I'm opening the can. It doesn't smell too bad, does it?"

"Rashid, it actually smells just like canned dog food usually does. My parents had a dog that sometimes got canned dog food, and it smelled just like that."

"What kind of dog was it?"

"It was a Husky named Pello."

"Okay, here it goes. Are you ready with the first-aid kit? I'm starting with half a spoonful."

"Bon appétit. How does it feel?"

"It actually tastes better than I expected. I'm having a little more."

"Hunger is the best seasoning, but don't eat too much. Stop now! Drink plenty of water and go lie down. Rest for a while, and we'll see how your body reacts."

"Don't you want to try it too?"

"I'll wait for now. Go lie down."

"Okay! Good night, sleep well."

"I'll try. Good night."

CHAPTER 9

"Rashid, are you awake? How are you feeling? How's your stomach?"

"Totally fine. In fact, I snuck back and ate almost everything in that can."

"That sounds good. I'll probably try some too, after a while. Can you tell me a bit about your upbringing in Afghanistan? What was it like?"

"We were fairly poor, but it was never bad enough that we went hungry. We had a small farm where we grew what we needed for ourselves, and we also had animals, two cows, sheep, goats, and quite a few chickens."

"What did you grow?"

"We grew potatoes, corn, onions, and various vegetables. We also had fruit trees, apples, plums, apricots, and a large mulberry tree. I love mulberries."

"Were there many of you in the family?"

"No, I was the only son, and when I was seven years old, I got a little sister, Samira. The birth was difficult, and my mother died that night. She bled to death, but my newborn sister survived. She made it. A neighbor woman who had given birth just a week earlier helped us and nursed Samira for a few months."

"So it was just the two of you, you and Samira?"

"Yes, my father had to take care of the two of us on his own. It was probably pretty tough for him, but the neighbors helped a little during the first few years after my mother died."

"That must have been very hard on him."

"When I was 14, a group of armed men came and tried to convince all the farmers in our village to start growing opium poppies. My father refused, so the men set fire to our house and all our outbuildings. But the worst part was that they took Samira with them when they rode off. That was the last time I saw her, and she was only seven years old."

"How horrible. That there are such cruel people ... "

"My father was devastated and blamed himself for not agreeing to the men's demands. He and I left the village, took some of our animals, and moved in with my uncle's family, who lived in another village, a day's walk away. My uncle's family had many children, seven of whom were still living at home. After a few days, my uncle said I was too old to live with them. His oldest son had moved to Iran and started working at a brick factory near Esfahan. That son sent part of his earnings home to his family. Now my uncle thought I should do the same, and after a few weeks, it was arranged for me to move to Iran and start working at the same brick factory as my cousin."

"Only 14 years old…"

"Yes, it was tough leaving my father and moving to another country, but I had no choice. My uncle's wife thought I should stay, but her opinion didn't carry much weight."

"Did you go to school at all when you lived in Afghanistan?"

"Yes, but not as much as I wanted to. I loved school, but it was a long walk, and my father often needed my help on the farm. I had a very good teacher, and I learned to read fairly quickly, even though I wasn't there very often. He even taught me a bit of English."

"Was that allowed?"

"I don't know, but he did it anyway. The teacher also let me borrow books to take home. He said I was smart and had an easy time learning new things. One time he told my father that I should spend more time at school and read more books. My father didn't understand the value of studying or why I liked school. He was illiterate and didn't think it was much of a problem."

"For me, it was the opposite. My parents thought that my sister and I were way too uninterested in schoolwork and studies. There was a lot of nagging about it in our house."

"What was your upbringing like otherwise?"

"I don't know if I want to talk about it."

"Why not?"

"It feels so unfair to you. You and I have had totally different circumstances. It feels wrong. My parents were diplomats, so we moved around the world. We lived in each country for a few years and went to the best and most expensive private schools available wherever we were. The Swedish government paid for it. To top it off, as I said earlier, neither my sister nor I were particularly interested in studying. There were so many other things that attracted us. I almost feel ashamed now."

"But it's not your fault the world is so unfair."

"Isn't it? I'm part of the system."

"What do you mean?"

"I tried smoking heroin once when I was young."

"And what are you trying to say with that?"

"Where does heroin come from? How is it made?"

"From opium ... "

"Exactly, and heroin wasn't free. Why do you think those armed men wanted your father to grow opium poppies?"

"Okay, I think I see what you're getting at."

"You have to think a few steps ahead."

"Why did you try smoking heroin?"

"I don't know. I wasn't sober at that party. Maybe it was just curiosity or peer pressure."

"Did it feel good? Did you get a high?"

"No, thank God, I felt awful. I threw up half the night and thought I was going to die."

"You were lucky you didn't get hooked."

"Yes, definitely."

"Fredrik, do you think you had a happy childhood and a good upbringing?"

"No, not really. Materially, we had everything, but I was probably often pretty unhappy. I felt like my parents were always working, and just when I'd settle into a place and make friends, we'd have to move to a new country. It created a kind of rootlessness, and I never felt at home anywhere. But it feels wrong to complain now that I know what your life was like."

"Fredrik, even if the world is full of injustices, we are at least equals in this special '*hotel*' where we are staying right now. We have the same standard of our rooms, we eat at the same restaurant, and we pick our meals from the same menu. So, what do you want to eat today?"

"Let me see ... hmm ... I think today I'll go with '*Canine Chef's Surprise*'."

"Such fancy words! It sounds like something very posh and very tasty, but today I'm so hungry I could probably eat dog food."

"I bet you could."

"What do you say, Fredrik? Should we celebrate the day by opening a can?"

"Now I think I'm brave enough. You don't seem to have suffered any serious harm from the dog food, at least not physically."

"What do you mean by that?"

"Now I'm hungry too. Let's head to the restaurant."

CHAPTER 10

"Rashid, is the brick factory you started working at in Iran the same place where you were accused of murdering your employer?"

"Yes, it is. I have only worked at one place ... one factory in Iran."

"Can you tell me what happened and why you are suspected of murder?"

"It was very hard work at the brick factory, but I earned more money than I spent. I could regularly send some of my wages home to my father."

"Did you and your cousin work together at this brick factory?"

"We did at first, even living in the same barracks. After a few months, though, he unfortunately had an accident that prevented him from continuing. He got one arm caught in a conveyor belt. His injuries were so severe that the arm had to be amputated. He was sent back to Afghanistan, and the last I heard, he was begging on the streets of Kabul. I kept working at the factory for over two years before I had to flee."

"What happened? Why are you suspected of murder?"

"As an undocumented guest worker, I couldn't send money home through a bank, but my employer arranged another solution. He had connections and made sure an envelope with dollar bills was sent to my father each month. I always included a letter describing how things were going but never mentioned how hard the work was or how poorly we were treated. I didn't want to upset my father. Since my father was illiterate, a man in the village would read my letters to him and help him send dictated replies. It was always a relief to read that he was doing relatively well."

"I understand that."

"After two years, a new guest worker arrived who had gone to the same school as I did. When we started talking, he mentioned my father's death, which shocked me, I had no idea. It turned out my father had died just three months after I'd left for Iran."

"That's awful! So you didn't know he had died and continued sending money. Who took your money, and who wrote the fake replies from your father?"

"That's what I wondered too. I went straight to my employer's office and angrily demanded an explanation. He said he would look into it but suggested someone in my home village must have tricked me."

"Did you believe him?"

"No, and what I didn't know then was that one of his daughters had overheard our conversation. She also heard her father calling someone right after I left his office. She overheard her father saying that I might have figured out what they had done and that I would need to be '*dealt with*'. '*Make sure he disappears for good*', she heard her father say to the person on the phone."

"That's horrible! Did she tell you all this?"

"Yes, she knocked on our barracks door late that same afternoon and asked me to come out so we could talk. She told me what she'd heard and urged me to leave immediately, convinced I would be killed otherwise. She also insisted I tell no one what she'd told me. '*My father will kill me*', she said."

"It was brave of her to tell you. Very courageous."

"Yes, but she was even braver than that."

"How so? What do you mean? Tell me."

"I told her I couldn't leave without getting back the money that had been stolen from me, and she said she might be able to help with that."

"Could she?"

"Late that evening, she came back to the barracks and asked me to come outside."

"Did she have the money?"

"She handed over a thick envelope full of dollar bills, saying she had taken it from her father's safe. I was surprised her father would give her access to the safe, but she said he hadn't. She had hidden her phone near the safe to secretly record her father entering the code. Fortunately, he opened it just before her phone's memory filled up."

"She was smart. But to have the courage ... "

"As soon as I got the money, I snuck away from the brick factory and spent the night half-sleeping in a shed near a café where truck drivers eat. The next day, I hid in the cargo of a truck headed to the port city of Bandar Abbas. I'd overheard the driver telling someone he was going there."

"Did the driver know you were hiding there?"

"No, but I was prepared to try bribing him if he discovered me."

"Was there a lot of money in the envelope?"

"Almost 5,000 US dollars!"

"Wow, was that really all the money your employer had taken from you?"

"No, but I think his daughter took every dollar she found in the safe."

"How long did the journey take?"

"About twelve hours, and the driver drove straight through with only two short breaks. I had two bottles of water, so I could stay in the cargo bed for the whole trip."

"Were you able to manage twelve hours without needing a restroom?"

"No, but I don't need to tell you all the details."

"What did you do when you arrived? What was the city called again?"

"Bandar Abbas. The truck stopped at the port, so I jumped out. By the dock was a ship that had just arrived with a cargo of rice from Pakistan. After a bit of negotiation with the captain, I arranged to travel back with the ship on its return trip to a Pakistani port."

"How much did you have to pay?"

"He agreed to 300 dollars, charging a bit extra since I had no passport. The captain liked that I could pay in US dollars, so I had no trouble getting on board."

"You were probably lucky to meet such an accommodating captain right then and there."

"Yes, I think I was lucky throughout my escape. The boat trip to Gwadar in Pakistan took two days, and the bus ride to Karachi took about eight hours. Everything went smoothly."

"So, your luck held out?"

"Yes, when I arrived in Karachi, I met Afghan refugees who helped me get the necessary identity documents and plane tickets."

"Forged IDs?"

"Yes, unfortunately. I know it's wrong, but what choice do you have when you're fearing for your life? Again, it was a huge help to have a bunch of dollars, so a little over three weeks after I left the brick factory outside Esfahan, I got off the plane at Stockholm Arlanda airport in Sweden. This was in January and it was very cold and dark."

"Was that your first time flying? It must have been a unique experience."

"Yes, my first flight was from Karachi to Istanbul, and the second was from Istanbul to Stockholm. It felt scary, exciting, and wonderful all at once."

"Why did you choose to come specifically to Sweden?"

"I remembered that my schoolteacher once said he dreamed of moving to Sweden someday. So, I thought it must be a good country."

"Do you know what happened to the brick factory owner's daughter?"

"No."

"I suspect things didn't turn out well for her. Sadly, it likely didn't end well at all."

"Why do you say that? Do you know something? Please tell me what you know!"

"I've tried to find out why you were sentenced to death in Iran so long ago, and the authorities there sent me a copy of the police report. It says that video surveillance footage from the factory owner's office shows you forcing your employer at gunpoint to open the safe and then coldly shooting him dead. It also states that they accidentally erased the footage when making a copy for the trial, but the local police had seen the video and witnessed the entire incident. Their testimony supposedly convinced the judge."

"What liars! And the daughter, does it mention anything about her in the report?"

"Yes, it says they found her drowned at the bottom of the family's pool. They assumed she had seen you near the crime scene, and when you noticed her, you believed she needed to be silenced, so you drowned her."

"My God, the lies they've made up. So I'm accused of two murders down there. Why have they concocted all of this?"

"I don't know. According to the police report, she was found with her school bag, filled with bricks."

"Poor girl. I feel guilty. What did I cause by saying I didn't want to leave without my money? Do they know who really shot my employer and who killed the daughter?"

"No, but one does wonder … "

"So terrible… she might have saved my life and paid with her own. Why did she do it? This is really hard to take in. I feel both guilty and grateful."

> "I don't think you should take any blame; it belongs with her father, he's the one who deceived you …"

"Yes, but still… poor girl."

CHAPTER 11

"Fredrik, you mentioned earlier that a few years ago, your parents drowned in New York and that thousands of others died simultaneously."

"Yes, it was over 8,000 people."

"How did the world react to that disaster? Did it affect people's views on the seriousness of climate change?"

"I was, of course, personally devastated by what happened, but from a global perspective, it wasn't actually considered one of the largest disasters. There have been many worse ones both before and after that flood."

"Wow, tell me more."

"For example, the US had a much deadlier disaster just north of Los Angeles a few years earlier. After months of no rain and extreme heat, there was a massive wildfire that, due to strong winds, developed into a system of intensely powerful firestorms that swept through places like Pasadena, Glendale, Burbank, and Santa Monica. I know these areas well since I once took some courses at a university in Santa Barbara, which is nearby."

"What kind of courses?"

"Writing courses, as I wanted to learn how to write for different types of media. The firestorms came so quickly and forcefully that very few could escape. Many people got into their cars, trying to drive away from the fire, but got stuck in traffic jams, allowing the flames to catch up. Since a large proportion of the cars were self-driving and their communication with traffic control systems collapsed due to damaged radio towers, these vehicles made crazy route choices. The cars couldn't get an overall picture of the traffic situation. When the events were later analyzed via satellite images, it was clear that many self-driving vehicles just drove around in circles."

"Oh no, were there a lot of fatalities?"

"Yes, over 30,000 people lost their lives in those fires. The firestorms consumed all the oxygen, so most people died from asphyxiation and suffocation before their bodies were burned. Those who survived were mostly the ones who had access to shelters or survival capsules and those who could avoid the jammed roads. Motorcycles and other fast two-wheelers saved some. Many people also managed to survive by heading out into the ocean. Other parts of the world, too, have suffered from deadly fires that have killed tens of thousands of people in Europe, Australia, Indonesia, India, and Brazil, to name a few."

"And how has it been with other types of climate disasters around the world?"

"In China, a massive dam broke after months of torrential rain filled it to the limit, and then a powerful earthquake weakened it so much that it suddenly collapsed. Over half a million people were killed downstream by the flooding."

"That's horrible. Such an enormous loss of life."

"In India, Pakistan, and Bangladesh, hundreds of thousands have also died from floods. In large parts of South America, deadly diseases have spread, especially new strains of dengue fever that have yet to be met with an effective vaccine or treatment. It's believed these deadly new diseases have been triggered by the collapse of the Amazon's interior ecosystem."

"Just think of the damage we humans have caused."

"Yes, and climate change has also caused the number of earthquakes to increase, making them stronger as well. Rising sea levels apparently affect the tensions between tectonic plates. Despite better early warning systems and new buildings constructed to withstand severe quakes, earthquake fatalities have skyrocketed in recent decades. Millions of lives have likely been lost."

"Frightening! You're painting a catastrophic picture of the world."

"I'm not painting a picture. It's just the grim reality. And I can tell you more. Africa is probably the continent hit hardest. Countless millions have died because the climate no longer follows normal patterns. Decades of failed crops mean traditional farming is no longer viable, and livestock die without enough water or food. Famine after famine has ravaged the continent."

"I knew there would be significant problems with the future climate, but that it would be this horrendous … "

"Altogether, an unimaginable number of people and animals around the world have lost their lives due to extreme climate changes over the past few decades."

"Hearing everything you've described almost makes you panic. Is there no hope? Is this the end of humanity?"

"Oh, there is hope. All these disasters finally made the world's population and its leaders realize that we share a common, deadly enemy: drastic climate change. We can no longer waste resources on wars between states when we face such a massively destructive enemy. This understanding is what gave the UN its new and crucial role today."

"Do people understand how serious the situation is?"

"No, not everyone. People react differently. A while ago, I started writing an article about this, though it's still unfinished. I tried to illustrate the different perspectives with a simplified model I called *ZEPREA*. Let's see if I remember what the letters in *ZEPREA* stand for."

The first letter, *Z*, is for the *Zombies* . These are the living dead who don't understand or refuse to understand how serious the climate threat is. They just carry on as usual."

The next letter, *E*, stands for the *Egoists* . They understand the situation but want to keep living comfortably for as long as possible without caring about the harm they cause others, the environment, or the climate. They ignore that their way of life is unsustainable and destroys things for future generations."

The third letter, *P*, stands for the *Pessimists* . They grasp the seriousness of the situation but believe it's beyond our control. *'It's all going to hell, but there's nothing I can do about it, so I won't do anything'*, they think."

"Some people are so annoyingly negative. The world would be much better if people used their energy to change what's wrong instead of just complaining."

"The next letter, *R*, is for a group I call the *Realists* . These people understand the severity of the situation but think it's almost impossible to turn things around. They focus on slowing the progression while preparing for the impending catastrophe. Their approach is almost palliative, like end-of-life care. They use mental training, medication, and other tools to ease their climate anxiety."

The next *E* stands for the *Extremists*. This group includes some religious groups where some even see the climate catastrophes as a positive sign. They don't want to do anything to stop the situation. They interpret it as the end of days, with their God soon returning to earth to save all believers. Thankfully, this group is in steep decline. Other extremists believe the world is overpopulated, seeing this as the root of all problems. They actively want to reduce the population as quickly as possible. Some extremists have even, horrifyingly, been discovered preparing for genocide."

"Is that true? I thought humanity had progressed to the point where genocide was only a thing of the past. Is there one more letter?"

"Yes, the last letter, *A*, stands for the *Activists*, now the dominant and fastest-growing group. Activists see that there is still hope for humanity if we actively work together to make the world more sustainable. AI-based decision-making support and future simulators have also helped show possible paths forward and inspired active involvement. I, of course, am part of the Activists."

"Tell me more about the Activists! There has to be hope. If everyone gives up, then things will definitely go to hell."

"Yes, but can we take a break first? It's been hard recounting all the disasters we've gone through. How about lunch, and we can continue afterward? Then we can talk about all the positive things happening."

"Sure, sounds good."

"What would you like for lunch? Anything special you're craving?"

"I think I'll go with the daily special today."

"Me too, it was good last time. What would you like to drink? Do you have a favorite drink?"

"Hard to choose… I think I'll go with water."

"Me too. Let's head to the restaurant."

CHAPTER 12

"Well, Fredrik, now I'm full and content."

"Really? Are you truly full and content?"

"No, but let's just say I'm more full than content. The dog food isn't as bad as I initially thought, so I can actually eat until I'm full, but there's a lot on my mind making me feel sad, shocked, and worried."

"What's on your mind?"

"Right now, I'm thinking a lot about what happened at the brick factory. Who was it that really shot the owner? Was there actually a surveillance video, and if so, what did it show? Could the video still exist? What really happened to the daughter, and did I somehow cause her death?"

"I told you not to blame yourself; you're not the one who did anything wrong."

"What about you, Fredrik? What are you thinking about?"

"I'm thinking a lot about what might have happened up there. How did it go for Sara? How did it go for everyone else? What caused that flash of light? Was it something local, or part of something bigger? There's a lot that worries me. I'm also considering whether we should try to get out of here, and if so, when."

"I think we should wait a bit longer, just to be safe."

"Yes, maybe that's best."

"Fredrik, you mentioned before lunch that there's also a lot of positive and hopeful news regarding the climate and the world situation. Could we talk about that now?"

> "Okay. The most important thing is the global realization that the situation is urgent and that all available resources must be used to try to turn things around. We also finally have a UN that can act forcefully and is really doing so."

"But what about the veto power? Superpowers like Russia, China, and the US have sometimes used the veto to block important decisions."

> "The veto power has been removed. It was a major obstacle to acting quickly for a safer, better world."

"How did that happen? How did the superpowers agree to give it up?"

> "It actually developed within the countries themselves. It became a strong public demand, starting in China, and then the other countries followed."

"In China? That's surprising. China is, or at least was, authoritarian, and public opinion didn't have much impact there. People didn't dare to speak out freely, right? Critics of the regime were usually seen as enemies of the state, enemies who had to be silenced."

"That, too, has fundamentally changed. A wave of democratization has swept across the world, even in China, Russia, and many other previously authoritarian countries."

"Wow, what caused this democratic shift?"

"It's largely thanks to *Confidonet*. People gained access to information that fairly accurately describes how the world really looks."

"*Confidonet*, what's that?"

"It resembles the old internet in terms of user experience, but on the new network, you can almost completely trust the information is correct. Not entirely, but nearly. The flood of fake information generated by AI back in the 2020s drove the development of Confidonet. At that time, you couldn't trust much of what was online; texts, images, voices, or videos… basically, nothing at all. It was very hard to tell what was true and what was fake. Enormous amounts of misinformation were spread by actors with malicious intent, both political and economic."

"Who developed Confidonet, and what makes it so trustworthy? Is it really possible to create a system with no security flaws at all?"

"Confidonet was initially developed within the academic community as a global collaborative project with open-source code. The UN quickly saw its advantages and supported its further development early on. The old internet still exists, but it now displays warning messages whenever potentially false information is shown, and there are plenty of those warnings. Most people now prefer Confidonet. One reason is that they don't have to worry about fake news, deceptive propaganda, scams, or other forms of trickery there."

"What characterizes this new network? What makes it so secure?"

"A crucial part is that anyone uploading information or sending messages has a verified identity and cannot remain anonymous. Rigorous and secure processes are used for identity verification. Various mechanisms also verify content, filtering out false or misleading information. AI algorithms analyze new content and cross-reference it against reliable sources. Additionally, strong encryption is used to prevent content from being tampered with in transit."

"That actually sounds pretty good, but is there any risk that we've ended up with a creepy surveillance society where no one dares to criticize or question authority?"

"There are still plenty of ways to express oneself anonymously, but on Confidonet, it's clear when information comes from an unverified user."

"But if the UN has now become so powerful, isn't it a bit frightening to have a supranational organization in control of almost everything? Are we now living in a society where '*Big Brother*' is watching?"

"Sure, in some ways, it's a surveillance society, but I think it's far better than before. Now, we have a large number of democratic states that, together and according to democratic principles, make decisions at the UN. Individual non-democratic countries or power-hungry leaders can no longer hold the rest of the world hostage as they did before, such as using nuclear threats to retain power."

"Speaking of that, what's the situation like with, say, North Korea? How are relations between North and South Korea?"

"Korea is no longer divided. There's only one Korea now, a free and democratic Korea. There are no longer any dictatorships obstructing the rest of the world."

"Has this shift to abolishing dictatorships been peaceful, or did it require force?"

"To some extent, military force was needed, but since the UN created a strong virtual defense force from the combined military resources of all member states, it became powerful enough that problematic states quickly became defenseless. The UN has also successfully implemented a policy where all conflict areas are made international territories under UN protection. Some of these areas have, after extended periods of peace, been reformed back into or connected to traditional states, usually after free democratic elections."

"What about military alliances like NATO and that Asian alliance where China, Russia, and India were involved? What role do they play today?"

"All those alliances have been dissolved. Historically, they played an important role, but now all major military resources are under the control of the UN."

"And the EU? Has its role changed?"

"It's the same story. The EU played an important role for several years, but that organization has now been dissolved as well. Now it's the UN that takes precedence. The EU evolved into a *Rich People's Club* that too often prioritized its own interests, and in the long run, that became unsustainable."

"That sounds like a hopeful development too."

"The biggest advantage is that global spending on war and conflict has been significantly reduced. Spending money on things that can, and maybe will be used to kill people and destroy infrastructure is not very smart."

"Amazing!"

"Those economic resources have instead been redirected to tackling climate issues. Additionally, the research and development resources previously used within the arms industry have now been redirected toward climate-related initiatives. This shift has allowed human ingenuity to be applied to something much more meaningful. In a way, the world has come to its senses and begun to prioritize in a much more sensible way than before."

"How has the weapons industry reacted? I imagine many people there see themselves as the losers in this change?"

"They've had to accept the shift, either by diversifying their operations or, in some cases, shutting down entirely. The UN has also banned private investments in companies with military orientations. Historically, there were even cases where venture capital deliberately fueled armed conflicts to try to increase the value of their investments. It's no longer possible to buy shares in companies tied to the weapons industry. You can't make money from death and destruction anymore."

"Fredrik, you mentioned earlier that there's been a wave of democratization sweeping the world. This sounds very interesting."

"Yes, in this area there has been a very positive development. "

"Tell me more about that? I've always seen the world as deeply undemocratic, and in many cases, the trend seemed to be heading in the wrong direction. The rich and powerful have used their strength to become even more powerful at the expense of the weak."

"Above all, it's the realization of the climate crisis's severity that has driven this change. Everyone has felt the impact of major climate disruptions, sparking enormous political engagement among many, at all levels and worldwide. Access to credible information via Confidonet and independent news channels has played a significant role. The UN's investment in improved public education worldwide has also been important. Many countries have done what Sweden has, abolishing specific election days held every few years and instead implementing individual annual voting. In Sweden, for example, you can vote for the parties and individuals you want to represent you in political assemblies on your birthday, with a 30-day window before or after. This system reduces the risk of someone using false information to stage a political coup or using exaggerated and sometimes false campaign promises to influence election results."

"How do political power shifts happen, then?"

"When certain threshold values in vote distribution are passed, and some time has elapsed, power shifts can occur. The idea is to avoid excessive political volatility, so a bit of inertia has been built into the system."

"Thank you, Fredrik, for this excellent lesson on the new political reality. It seems there's still some hope for humanity, after all. But now I actually need to visit the restroom, I think the dog food has worked its way through."

CHAPTER 13

"Fredrik, I've been thinking a lot about that flash of light you mentioned."

"Okay, what are your thoughts?"

"I'm pretty sure it came from a nuclear explosion. I'm almost certain."

"It's certainly possible that a nuclear explosion could have caused the flash, I'll agree with that. But what makes you so sure, or almost sure, that it was specifically a nuclear explosion? I think there could be other explanations."

"Well, since both your ComU and my ankle monitor no longer work, it was probably an electromagnetic pulse that knocked them out. Nuclear weapons emit such a pulse. I read a book at the cabin about the nuclear threat, and it explained the effects of an EMP, an electromagnetic pulse. Apparently, it can disable electronics over a vast distance."

"How do you know your ankle monitor isn't working? I noticed you had one on when I dragged you out of the elevator, and Sara also shouted something about the ankle monitor when she shoved us into the elevator, but how on earth do you know it's not working?"

"The ankle monitor they put on me every time I leave the prison building, like when it's time for a walk, has a special information function. When they attach and lock it around my ankle, it always automatically plays the same recorded warning message. The voice says that if I leave the allowed area or attempt to remove it without using a key, a sedative will be injected, making me unable to move. When we ended up down here, the monitor should have reacted and sedated me."

"Ah, that's why Sara shouted '*ankle monitor*' at the elevator. She was probably going to get a key to prevent that from happening."

"You mean she couldn't follow us down because she was trying to help me, that she was going to get the key?"

"Maybe … "

"Oh no, now I feel guilty again."

"But wait, maybe the monitor's electronics are still working. You were completely unconscious and couldn't move. Maybe you were injected… maybe it wasn't the hit to the head that knocked you out … "

"You can actually help me figure out if it works or not."

"How? I'm not going to try to take it off you."

"No, no… there's another way. There's a test button near the lock. If you press the button, an LED light should blink a few times. I've heard the guards mention it. I've never seen it blink myself, for obvious reasons. Give me your hand, and I'll show you where the button is."

"Okay, I found it. I'm pressing and pressing, but nothing's happening."

"Try holding it down a bit longer."

"It still won't blink."

"That's our answer; it must have been a nuclear explosion."

"Maybe, but there are other things that could have disabled the electronics."

"Like what?"

"The elevator was slowed by very strong permanent magnets, since the brakes have to work even if the power's out. Sara explained how it all functions. She also mentioned that when she tested the elevator herself once, her ComU stopped working, the magnets disabled it. Sensitive electronics are supposed to be placed in a special electronically shielded box in the elevator. I didn't see any such box when we jumped in, but then, I wasn't even thinking about what she'd told me earlier. Everything happened so fast."

"Okay, then maybe I can't be so certain about it being a nuclear explosion?"

CHAPTER 14

"Rashid, I've been thinking about something. When we get out of here ... "

"If (!) we get out of here ... "

"You're usually so positive, but okay ... If (!) we get out, I don't think it will be especially difficult to show that you're innocent of the terrorist attack in Norway. Plus, you should be cleared of all suspicions about the murder or murders at the brick factory. Then you'll be entitled to some restitution and compensation for having been imprisoned for so many years for something you didn't do. You'll receive substantial compensation."

"Great, then maybe they can make me twenty years younger, bring Marie back from the dead, and give me new eyes."

"All that might be difficult, but besides financial compensation, would you like to have your vision back?"

"What a question! Of course, but it's impossible. There's nothing left of my eyes, absolutely nothing. Do you mean they should transplant eyes from someone deceased or some poor animal? Maybe they can find a few impoverished donors who would be willing to sell me one of their eyes? No thanks, I'd rather stay blind."

"None of that's an option. It's proven extremely difficult to transplant entire eyes despite all the other advances made in transplantation technology. There are better methods to try to give you your sight back."

"And how would that work?"

"This is a technique that already exists and works. A large number of thin electrodes are implanted in the visual cortex at the back of the neck. The blind person wears glasses with two digital cameras for stereoscopic vision, as it's sometimes called. The cameras send the image information to an implant near the visual center in the neck. The implant re-codes the information from the cameras into a customized pattern of electrical impulses sent to the electrodes. The brain interprets these signals as images. The precise placement of the electrodes in the cortex is important, and the surgery is done with a precision robot. Vision training after the operation is done with advanced AI support. The implanted device then holds the customized translation of the camera signals into the pattern of impulses sent to the cortex."

"Wow, what a detailed description. How do you know so much about that technology? I'm impressed with your knowledge."

"A childhood friend of mine worked many years ago as a landmine clearer. On a mission for the UN in Somalia, the unthinkable happened. Despite all precautions, a mine exploded directly in her face, and the blast was so powerful that the visor of her protective helmet shattered, and she lost vision in both eyes. Two years ago, she underwent one of those operations, and she now has reasonably good vision. Despite her handicap, she's one of the most life-loving people I know."

"So that actually works?"

"Absolutely. It's been around for a few years now, and there are thousands of users around the world. It still works best in black and white, and the resolution isn't very high yet, but it works. Users can navigate relatively easily, read newspapers and books, watch movies, browse the internet, and even fairly easily recognize people they meet."

"Impressive!"

"Plus, there are some advantages compared to ordinary human vision."

"Really, like what?"

"You have autofocus, you can have light-enhancing cameras, so your night vision becomes better than that of normal-sighted people, and you can have voice-activated zoom."

"Real spy gadgets. Are there any risks with that type of surgery?"

"There are always risks, I guess. I don't think they're very large, and maybe they're worth taking if you can regain your vision, right? I might be able to arrange for you to meet my childhood friend. Then she can share her experiences with you."

"That would be interesting ... if we ever get out of here."

"Rashid, it's important to stay positive and never give up."

"My brain also suffered other injuries after the attack. It wasn't just my eyes that were destroyed when I was shot. Can my brain handle more trauma?"

"I can't answer that. I don't have enough medical knowledge."

"Then there's also the question of whether you even want your vision back, depending on what it's like out there or up there."

"What do you mean?"

"Do you want to see the misery if everything is ruined, if everything beautiful in the world is destroyed? Have we had a third world war with nuclear weapons? In a book I read a long time ago, it said that after such a war, it would be so awful that the survivors would probably envy the dead. Maybe the sighted would even envy the blind?"

CHAPTER 15

"Rashid, what's that strange noise? What are you doing?"

"I'm trying to open the steel door, but I haven't yet managed to turn the lower knob. It's very stiff."

"Wait! Stop! You can't make decisions on your own and do things that could put us in mortal danger without us discussing together the pros and cons it might bring. There might be high levels of radioactive radiation, toxic gas, or something else life-threatening on the other side of the door."

"It might be more dangerous to continue to stay down here."

"That could be true, but we need to talk through the different options together to try to make the best decisions. I might have thoughts and ideas you haven't thought of, and you might bring up important aspects I've missed. To assess different options in the best way, we need to make use of our shared experiences ... our shared expertise ... right?"

"Sorry. You're probably right. I don't know what came over me."

"Why did you want to open the door?"

"I wanted to check what's on the other side."

"We might need to do that soon, but right now, I don't think the situation here is so urgent. If, for example, there is radioactive radiation out there, it will decay over time, so it's best if we wait as long as possible. Why are you in such a hurry? Do you see any reason why we should rush out?"

"No, not really. I don't know why I got the idea to try to open the door. Maybe I'm just frustrated with our limited diet. I'm getting really tired of that dog food. The one-sided diet may have made it so that I can no longer think clearly."

"Sometimes situations arise where you need to make quick decisions and rely on gut feeling, but if you have the chance, it's usually better to consider as many aspects as possible before deciding what to do."

"Yes, that sounds like a good idea, but can't that take a lot of time and energy? If you think for too long, you might miss certain opportunities. The train may have left the station."

"It depends on the situation. Nowadays, we often have AI to help, which makes it much easier to make good decisions."

"Yeah, yeah ... but not here and now. How could artificial intelligence in another context help us make better decisions?"

"I can give you an example. My grandfather was a medical doctor, and he worked as one well into his seventies. Over time, he became quite experienced, and when someone came with unusual symptoms, he could often see parallels to some of the thousands of patients he had encountered before. He would also take time to look over a few pages of the patient's records and flip through the medical literature he had access to. He probably also looked at current test results. That's how he tried to make a diagnosis. Today, doctors use AI support. The entire patient's record (which can be very extensive) and numerous test results and analyses can be compared in seconds with the histories of millions of patients worldwide. With this foundation and access to all relevant medical literature, the system can quickly make a highly accurate diagnosis. It's a huge difference."

"But a human doctor can also see changes in a patient's skin color, the way they talk, and a lot of other things."

"AI systems can also interpret images and sounds."

"You really like artificial intelligence. When I was new in Sweden, there was a lot of talk about AI, but if I remember correctly, it was mostly about problems. People thought AI would take a lot of jobs and make people unemployed. AI had also started to be used for cheating on school assignments, so there was a fear that school grades wouldn't give a fair picture. As I remember, AI was associated almost exclusively with problems."

"Was it really like that? Was there such a negative view?"

"So, how did it turn out? Did it cause mass unemployment and let the *'wrong people'* get into desirable educational programs?"

"In the beginning, it was heading that way, but it changed fairly quickly. The challenges of climate change were and are so great that it wasn't acceptable to not have every person contribute in some way. It would be an irresponsible waste of human resources. Once upon a time, you could be sentenced to *community service* for certain crimes. That term used to have a negative connotation, but nowadays, community service is something that everyone is expected to do, and essentially everyone does, at least a few hours a week. If, for example, someone's job is automated and they lose it, maybe replaced by some kind of robot, they perform community service until they take or are given another job. Unemployment essentially no longer exists. Now that there's meaningful work for everyone, crime rates have also dropped significantly. There's just not as much room for alternative *'career paths'*, and by that, I mean criminal careers."

"Are you paid for community service?"

"No, not for the service itself, but the means-tested support for people who don't have enough to support themselves independently is conditional on their fulfilling their civic duty."

"And what happens if you refuse?"

"That somebody refuses? It doesn't happen often, but society usually handles it on a case-by-case basis. Sometimes it's psychological issues, in which case it leads to healthcare interventions. In other cases, it might be criminals who don't feel like participating, and then it becomes a case for the police and the justice system."

"What does community service involve?"

"Oh, there's an endless need for services that society benefits from."

"Can you give me some examples?"

"For example, you might help grow vegetables for schools, hospitals, and nursing homes. Maybe you take the elderly or those with mobility issues on outings, supervise recess, patrol neighborhoods in the evenings, plant trees, clear weeds, clean solar panels ... There's so much that needs doing. Plus, people don't do well without meaningful things to do."

"Can someone refuse to contribute in that way?"

"Refuse, why would they?"

"Let's take an extreme case. If someone is totally paralyzed, they can't help out that way."

"Well, I actually know someone who's totally paralyzed but still does her community service. She's the sister of a colleague who lives in Alingsås. She's completely paralyzed and can't even speak, but she can control a computer with her eye movements and, among other things, write texts. Her regular job is as a children's book author, and she writes fantastic stories. A few hours a week, she also does community service. She's part of a group that, for the UN, performs ranger services for a threatened rainforest area in Brazil. Satellite images of the area are scanned by AI, but this group also helps review assigned image frames. They look for logging, fires, or anything unusual. If she sees something suspicious in an image, she blinks in a certain way, and then others follow up more closely and sound the alarm if needed. She really appreciates being able to participate in something so meaningful."

"But if she's creating fantastic stories, that work is already really meaningful."

"Absolutely! She has two very meaningful jobs. When needed, she also assists the organization *Missing People* in trying to find missing persons. Then, she usually scans drone images. She recently found a little five-year-old boy who had wandered off in a dense energy forest outside Örebro. She has a trained eye."

"Was he alive?"

"Yes, he was, but he was very sad and very hungry."

"What about the cheating in schools?"

"Oh right, but grades have been completely abolished, so any potential cheating isn't an issue."

"So, how do they select people for various educational programs?"

"There are entrance exams and aptitude tests for everything, both for higher education and jobs. These tests measure only what is relevant for that particular education or job."

"Doesn't that involve a tremendous amount of testing? Do they really have the resources for that?"

"Much of what can be considered general testing is handled by an independent national testing organization, done very resource-efficiently with AI and robotics."

"What does general testing mean?"

"It could be testing language skills, physical strength, mental resilience, concentration, subject knowledge in areas like social studies, mathematics, statistics, biology, programming, etc."

"Why did they stop using grades as a selection tool? Was it because of cheating with AI?"

"Partly, but there was a lot of cheating even before AI. Grades were also assigned differently at different schools, and there was favoritism and even bribery that complicated things. In a global world with people who've attended schools in other countries with different grading systems, interpreting and valuing those grades also became difficult. Overall, relying on grades as a selection tool became unsustainable. It's much better to test what's relevant for each education or job."

"If you fail a test, is that it? Are you out?"

"No, you can retake the tests pretty much as many times as you want. People gain experience, they mature and continue to develop new skills. Naturally, you should get new chances."

"If you take a test a lot of times, isn't there a risk you'll pass just because you've memorized the answers?"

"No, because the questions and tasks are created on the spot by AI and are unique for each test and individual. The variations are practically limitless."

"Sounds like a good system."

"That national testing organization has another important and very valuable function as well."

"Tell me."

"The organization handles both counseling and testing."

"Counseling? In what way?"

"It provides both study and career counseling. Based on your test results, your interests, your aptitude for different things, and so on, it can suggest suitable studies and self-study options, as well as job recommendations."

"Is this also AI-based?"

"Of course, no human could manage the necessary overview of such a vast area to give good tips and really good recommendations."

CHAPTER 16

"Rashid, I've seen the light."

"That almost sounds religious. Have you had an epiphany, or have you figured out the meaning of life?"

"I've seen the light from your ankle monitor."

"Oh! When? Tell me!"

"During your last sleep cycle, you snored so badly that I couldn't sleep myself. I got up to go close the door to your room, and just as I was about to do it, there were three flashes from inside the room. There was about a second's pause between the flashes. The light allowed me to make out the outlines of the room and of you. I could also see that the light flashes came from your ankle monitor."

"Were there only three flashes?"

"Yes, there were just three that I saw. I sat down on the bed opposite yours and stared into the darkness toward you ... toward your snoring ... for at least half an hour, but I couldn't make out any more flashes. It was just total darkness. I also sneaked forward and checked with my hands to make sure you hadn't pulled anything over your foot that could cover the light."

"Strange, only three flashes ... "

"Yes, and while I was sitting there, I thought about possible explanations."

"And what did you come up with?"

"There's something called self-repairing electronics."

"What's that?"

"Redundancy is built into the technical solution, so if one part stops working, other parts automatically take over the function. But the switchover usually happens lightning-fast, so I don't think that's why the ankle monitor woke up. Another explanation could be that your ankle monitor suddenly got contact with some network that triggered these flashes, but I'm just guessing now … "

"Maybe it was some kind of death throes when the battery in the ankle monitor ran out."

"That actually sounds like the most likely explanation. After staring into the darkness toward the sound of your snoring for quite some time, I went back to my room and tried to emergency charge my ComU by rolling the scroll wheel back and forth on the floor. I kept at it until I almost got a cramp in my arm."

"Did you get the device going?"

"No, it was as dead as before."

"Fredrik, you said earlier that a ComU is far more advanced than a smartphone."

"Did I say that?"

"I think you mentioned earlier that the new devices have functionalities light-years ahead of what the old phones could do."

"I might have said that … "

"Can you explain what's different?"

"I'll try. Above all, they've become much better at interacting with the immediate surroundings and with the human body."

"How so?"

"If you use a smart toilet, the kind that can analyze urine and feces, the analysis results, which cover hundreds of health markers, can be communicated to your ComU and processed with other health data your ComU monitors. If the system detects something abnormal, it gives you recommendations on how to act."

"Where can you find a smart toilet like that?"

"Many people have one at home; they're also quite common at workplaces, hotels, and public restrooms."

"Ugh, that sounds creepy! Such an invasion of personal privacy! Information about potential health issues might be something you want to keep to yourself, and a smart toilet could also reveal if you've taken drugs."

"That's why it's all voluntary. You choose if you want to use that type of toilet and if you want to activate the function. Many people think the benefits outweigh the drawbacks. Personally, I always have the function activated."

"Good that there's a choice."

"Another function I almost always keep activated is voice and movement analysis."

"What does that mean?"

"When I talk, my device analyzes how I speak. If, for example, I start slurring, it might be a sign of a stroke or some other health issue."

"I don't think I'd want that function. What about movement analysis?"

"It's a similar function. It can trigger an alert if my movement pattern suddenly deviates from the norm, which could also be due to a health problem."

"I suppose it's some kind of AI that processes information about both your voice and movements."

"You guessed it!"

"I'm not at all surprised."

"I can give another example. If I go into a restaurant I've never been to before, my ComU can answer questions about where the bathrooms are, what's on the menu, and whether I'm allergic to any dishes. It can also alert me if there's a favorite dish of mine on the menu and whether previous guests enjoyed it. If it's an outdoor seating area, it can also warn if rain is on the way. So, I don't have to actively search for information or input my preferences. My ComU knows me, knows what I prefer, and is aware of the environment around me."

"Sounds convenient."

"Yes, that is a very useful. "

"You mentioned it can also interact with the human body. How so?"

"Before I explain how that works, maybe I should mention that there are different types of ComU devices."

"Okay."

"The one I have with me now is a handheld model that can be kept in a pocket. It's quite similar to the '*antique*' smartphones you're probably familiar with."

"Limited experience, I'd say."

"Then there are a variety of models with different sizes and capabilities. Some have one or multiple screens, some lack screens and are typically controlled by voice. Some can be worn on the wrist, some around the neck as jewelry, or attached to clothing as a brooch. Many prefer to have their ComU integrated with glasses. There are also models that are implanted in the body."

"Wow! So, are those implanted models the ones that can interact with the body?"

"No, actually, all models can do that if you've given permission for it."

"You'll have to explain that a bit more."

"For those who want it, you can have a number of small electronic sensors implanted or injected into your body."

"Ugh, that sounds creepy. What's the point of that?"

"Those sensors can, for instance, monitor heart rate, blood pressure, body temperature, oxygen saturation in the blood, glucose levels, and other factors that can alert you if you have a medical problem."

"Do you get a notification on your ComU?"

"That can happen, but in many cases, the information is first sent over the network for more advanced analysis."

"Why is that?"

"To perform a really good analysis, sometimes you need more computing power and quicker access to large amounts of data than your ComU can handle. If you're seriously ill, help can also be dispatched to your location."

"They send an ambulance?"

"Yes, or a drone with the kind of help or support you urgently need."

"It all sounds advanced and expensive."

"Maybe advanced, but this sensor system actually makes healthcare cheaper."

"How so?"

"By detecting medical problems early, you can often take measures early enough to avoid more advanced and thus more expensive care later on. An unhealthy lifestyle, with poor eating habits and too much sitting, can also be detected, and the person can get recommendations to change their habits."

"Isn't that really invasive?"

"Of course, but it's also why it's optional to have those sensors implanted."

"That information must be very interesting for insurance companies. They could see if it's a bad deal to let someone take out a life insurance policy, right? Some people might not be able to get insurance at all."

"That whole concept of life, health, and accident insurance is almost a thing of the past. Most countries now have a strong social safety net, so you don't need insurance."

"Do you have a lot of sensors in your body?"

"Not too many. There's a history in my family of several people having strokes at an early age, so due to that hereditary risk, I have several sensors implanted in my head. These sensors keep track of my brain waves. There are patterns that can appear in the early stages of a stroke. If that happens to me, I'd get a recommendation to go to the hospital for further examinations and preventive treatment. Naturally, I also have sensors for blood pressure, heart rate, and body temperature."

"Do you have to go to the hospital sometimes to change batteries?"

"No, there are several ways to handle power supply for implanted electronics. One way is to charge the batteries wirelessly through induction. Many new beds and seating furniture have charging functions that automatically charge implanted electronics in people who lie or sit in them."

"Impressive, but you mentioned there are several methods."

"Yes! Another way is metabolic power supply, where the energy indirectly comes from the food you eat. A third method is to harness the energy from your normal bodily movements. The electronics have become so energy-efficient that it doesn't take much to keep them running."

"When using induction, aren't you exposed to a lot of electric fields that could be harmful?"

"No, the charging functions detect exactly where the electronics are in the body and direct targeted electromagnetic fields precisely to the right points and only in the limited amount needed."

"But if you've been lying in an old-fashioned bed for a while and haven't sat in any newer furniture with a charging function, isn't there a risk that the electronics stop working?"

"Well, this electronics usually isn't absolutely vital, and you also get an early warning message when charge levels start getting low. Then you have plenty of time to fix the problem."

"They seem to have thought of everything."

"Yes, it works really well."

"If someone abuses alcohol or drugs, don't the sensors detect that, too?"

"They could certainly do that, but drug problems have almost entirely disappeared from society."

"What? How did that happen? That sounds like an incredible development."

"Of course, there are people who want to, and sometimes even need to, escape reality, but nowadays, there's free help available."

"Free happy pills?"

"No, they also use electronics and AI here. Through special helmets, you can direct electromagnetic pulses to parts of the brain and stimulate various centers. This way, you can achieve effects similar to those from drugs like alcohol and various narcotics. These helmets are also often used for pain relief for certain illnesses, during childbirth, and for surgeries."

"Can you also use the helmets for fun?"

"Absolutely, that's why these helmets are sometimes called '*party hats*'. The advantage of this type of virtual intoxication is that you usually don't suffer from terrible morning-after symptoms or withdrawal problems. Some withdrawal effects can occur, but they're not nearly as intense as with traditional intoxicants."

"The expression '*happy as a clam*' just took on a whole new meaning for me."

CHAPTER 17

"Fredrik, do you know you talk in your sleep?"

"Oh no, I knew I used to do that when I was younger, but I thought I'd stopped. What did I say? Did I say something dumb?"

"You called out '*Dolores ... Dolores*' and then mumbled something I couldn't understand. I don't even know what language you were mumbling in. Who is Dolores, anyway? Is she your girlfriend from Hawaii, the one you've never met?"

"Girlfriend might be a bit of a stretch ... but Dolores is the woman in Hawaii I've been in touch with a lot online."

"I think your relationship sounds really interesting and intriguing."

"She's originally from Mexico but now lives and works in Hawaii."

"Didn't you say before that she works with space research?"

"Exactly. She's a researcher connected to the *Keck Observatory*, and her field is the conditions for life on exoplanets. Simply put, she's looking for signs of life on planets outside our solar system."

"How did you get in touch with her?"

"I've always been interested in the possibility of life on other planets. A long time ago, she was on a TV program about extraterrestrial life in the universe, and for some reason, her name stuck with me, *Dolores Gonzales.*"

"How did you manage to contact her?"

"I just searched for her name online, and after a while, I found her email address. It wasn't easy, given how many people named Dolores Gonzalez there are, but I finally found one who was an astronomer and figured it had to be her."

"Tell me more!"

"I emailed her, sharing my interests, who I was, and a few specific questions related to the TV show's content. I didn't expect much, but just a few hours later, she replied with a short message."

"What did she say in her reply? Tell me! I'm really curious now."

"She asked if we could video chat since it'd be easier to answer my questions interactively. She suggested we connect via Confidonet, which we did almost right away."

"Wow!"

"This happened around midsummer, and I was working from a little cabin I'd rented outside Svolvær in Lofoten, up in the northern part of Norway. It was the midnight sun up there, and stunningly beautiful. The sun was shining even though it was late in the evening. Meanwhile, Dolores was having an early lunch on her porch on Big Island, Hawaii. The time difference is 12 hours."

"So, she was in the afternoon sun in Hawaii, and you were in the midnight sun in the far north of Norway?"

"Well, actually, there was no sun where she was. She lives outside a town called Hilo, one of the rainiest places in the US. Big Island has a rainy side and a sunny side. She lives where it rains almost 300 days a year, though usually not constantly, sunshine peeks through now and then. She lives right by the ocean; beautiful views, lots of greenery, palms, tropical plants, flowers, and lots of rain. I'd love to visit her someday."

"How did the video chat go?"

"Amazingly well! We started talking about the conditions for life in the universe, but soon the conversation drifted, and we ended up talking about everything under the sun. How long do you think we talked?"

"Since you're asking, I'm guessing it went on for a while. I'd say several hours."

"Nearly four hours! It was insane; we connected right away. I showed her the view from my cabin, and she gave me a tour of her garden. We were both fascinated by what we saw, but the most interesting part was when we got into philosophical questions about life. Since that day, we chat almost daily, though only about half an hour at a time."

"So, you found your soulmate online. Are you two in love?"

"How can you tell? We haven't talked about it in those terms, but I think we both appreciate each other's presence in the virtual world."

"Do you miss the chance to contact her now?"

"What do you think? Of course! Dolores and I recently got equipment that lets us go on semi-virtual outings together remotely. It's been really wonderful."

"What kind of equipment is it?"

"It's something called '*Walk-By-Me Drones*'. When Dolores takes me on an outing, she has a drone that flies at my eye level beside her, representing me. I wear a VR headset, and when I move my head, the drone next to her adjusts accordingly. I control the drone's viewpoint with my head movements, able to look up, down, or around. It feels like we're on a walk together, side by side."

"Are you also at the same time walking at home with a similar drone flying or virtually '*walking*' beside you?"

"No, that'd be too chaotic. Only one of us at a time controls the walk and decides where to go. It can be walking …or other forms of movement."

"Other forms?"

"Yes, I have walked with Dolores along beautiful beaches, rode horses with her up in the mountains and even kayaked, all while sitting in a chair at home and just moving my head."

"Cool!"

"Being able to control the viewpoint and hear perfect sound makes the experience incredibly immersive."

"Isn't the buzzing sound of the drone annoying?"

"What buzzing? Today's drones have extremely quiet rotor blades, designed with sound-dampening features inspired by owl wings. Owls are known for flying almost silently due to the sound-dampening properties of their fringed feathers. The latest electric motors are also extremely quiet, and with the VR headset's active noise cancellation, you hardly notice any drone noise. I've taken Dolores on walks in Swedish forests, and she's commented on the beautiful birdsong."

"Wow, drones have become that quiet?"

"Besides cameras and microphones, the drone has sensors that measure temperature, wind, and humidity. This information is used to control tiny fans on the receiver's end, which blow air at just the right temperature and humidity across the face through the VR headset, giving the receiver an amazing sense of being where the sender is. There's also an infrared heating element to enhance the experience."

"What about smells?"

"The drones and headsets we got don't transmit smells. There are models that do, but they're significantly heavier and quite expensive, so we opted out of that feature. Plus, battery life is much shorter with the smell feature. With our equipment, you can virtually walk together for over an hour before needing a battery change."

"What else has she shown you in Hawaii?"

"Oh, tons! She's taken me to the Keck Observatory at over 4000 meters near the top of Mauna Kea. There was a lot of snow up there that day. We also visited an active volcano that's been erupting for decades. It was amazing to stand near a stream of red, molten lava, the infrared heating really got to work. My face felt hot!"

"Impressive!"

"She also took me along when she and some colleagues kayaked off the point where explorer James Cook was reportedly killed by locals. A pod of dolphins swam around us, jumping and playing. It felt like I was actually in one of the kayaks; it was fantastic. I could hear the splashing of dolphins all around me. The sound and picture quality were outstanding, and I even felt virtual water splashes, drops running down my VR glasses. We didn't land but paddled close to the monument where it's believed James Cook died in the late 1700s."

"It was 1779; he was stabbed in the back, according to a book I read about it."

"Rashid, you're well-read and seem to have a great memory for details."

"Apparently, during the chaos after a cultural misunderstanding, several people were killed on both sides, among the Hawaiians and Cook's crew. Before that, they'd had a mutually good and peaceful relationship."

"Dolores mentioned that she and her colleagues sometimes consider themselves cosmic explorers. They see James Cook as both an inspiration and a cautionary example. They want to be curious but also careful."

"Careful so no alien comes along and stabs them in the back … ?"

"No, it's not like that. They want to be careful about how they interpret what they discover and how they communicate their findings."

"What have you shown Dolores? Have you taken her on any other virtual outings besides forest walks with bird songs?"

"She's been on plenty of tours in both Sweden and Norway with me. Like me, she loves Lofoten, but she also enjoys mountain hikes. We've sailed together in the Stockholm archipelago, too."

"I really think you should go to Hawaii and visit her. Can't you just fly there?"

"Flying isn't so easy nowadays. The UN only allows fossil-free flights, and they're quite expensive, especially for long-distance. I've looked into an alternative; boat from Copenhagen to New York, then train across the US to Los Angeles, and finally another boat trip to Hawaii. It's much cheaper than flying but would take around three weeks."

"Are the boats fossil-free, too?"

"Of course, they have to be under UN regulations. The boats are hydrogen powered, so the only emission is water."

"Well, then, just book the trip."

"Rashid, do you really think we'll ever get out of here?"

"Stay positive, Fredrik, never give up."

"You're right. Giving up means it's really over."

"How's Dolores's research going? Have they found life on other planets?"

"They did some years ago. The evidence is compelling. Simple forms of life have even been found within our own solar system. But they've also found clear signs of life on a number of exoplanets many light-years away."

"How can they detect life on celestial bodies so incredibly far away?"

"There are different methods. One common one is spectroscopy, where they analyze light that has passed through an exoplanet's atmosphere, light coming from a distant source beyond the planet. Through this analysis, they can identify specific chemical compositions that may be associated with life. Certain molecules, like ozone, methane, and carbon monoxide, can hint at biological activity."

"Have they found any advanced life forms?"

"According to Dolores, they're close to presenting evidence that there were once higher life forms on other planets."

"How so?"

"They've developed methods to show atmospheric changes over time on planets, similar to studying tree rings on an old tree here on Earth. By examining how the tree rings grew over time, you can see how the climate changed throughout its life. I haven't fully understood how they do it with exoplanets, even though Dolores has explained it to me several times. It involves months-long measurements of various carbon isotopes and an extrapolation of the results, though I might be remembering it wrong. Dolores did say they've closely studied the atmosphere around a particular exoplanet 58 light-years away that resembles Earth in many ways. It's at about the same distance from its host star as we are from the Sun, it has an Earth-like orbit, and surface gravity similar to ours. They've managed to calculate atmospheric data over about a 3,000-year period. During that time, they observed that enormous amounts of fossil material were burned, causing a rapid increase in carbon dioxide levels in the atmosphere. This, in turn, heated up the atmosphere, making it impossible for any life forms similar to ours to survive."

"Yikes, that sounds eerily like what's happening on Earth now."

"Exactly, and that's why they want to be extra careful about how they interpret this information and how they present it. They don't want to cause unnecessary panic on our planet. It could have been an advanced life form that caused the problem, much like we humans have on Earth, but there may be other explanations."

"Like what?"

"If there was plant life similar to ours on that planet, volcanic eruptions or lightning-like electrical discharges could have ignited fossil material that burned or smoldered for hundreds or thousands of years. Rashid, I really want to emphasize that this is just a wild guess based on things Dolores has loosely speculated about and mentioned to me. I may have also misinterpreted or misunderstood what she shared."

"What about intelligent life? Have they seen any signs of it?"

"What do you mean by intelligent life?"

"Something like human life or other highly evolved life?"

"Do you think human life counts as highly evolved intelligence when you think about the mess we've made?"

"Fredrik, you know what I mean."

"They've made observations that might indicate intelligent thought and extremely advanced planning."

"Fascinating. Tell me more!"

"Another Earth-like exoplanet, about 114 light-years away, with an atmosphere similar to ours, appeared to be at risk of colliding with a massive asteroid. Based on astronomical calculations, it would have struck the exoplanet with such force that it would likely have lost the ability to support any form of life. Astronomers worldwide began intensely monitoring the planet, calculating the exact time of impact. But to everyone's surprise, the collision didn't happen."

"Did they miscalculate?"

"No, it turns out the asteroid's path changed just before the expected impact."

"How did that happen?"

"This is where theories about higher intelligence and advanced planning come in. A number of smaller asteroids collided with the larger one, altering its path in a way that could only be described as cosmic billiards at a world-class level. Many astronomers argue it's impossible for it to have happened randomly. They believe there must have been some form of advanced intelligence behind it, ensuring the smaller asteroids were nudged precisely."

"Does Dolores believe that, too?"

"She estimates there's more than a 90 percent probability that a higher extraterrestrial intelligence planned and executed the whole thing."

"So, she believes intelligent life exists out there!"

"That it might have existed ... "

"What do you mean by '*might have existed*'? I don't quite follow."

"If that cosmic event took place 114 light-years away, we only know that life probably existed there 114 years ago. If our Sun went out, we wouldn't know for about eight minutes since it takes that long for sunlight to reach Earth. Similarly, it takes 114 years for us to see changes in something 114 light-years away."

"Yeah, but if there was intelligent life on that exoplanet 114 years ago, doesn't it stand to reason it's still there? Don't you think that's logical?"

"But if the asteroid hadn't been diverted, maybe things would be different. In this case, any potential life might have been wiped out."

"Has this almost certainty that we're not alone in the universe been officially announced?"

"No, so far it's only being discussed among a small group of astronomers, and Dolores said she was very hesitant about sharing the discovery with me. She thinks they need to carefully consider how to handle this information before going public."

"Why?"

"They need to be absolutely certain that the observations are correct and that the conclusions make sense. Additionally, they need to consider if society needs to be prepared in some way for such a dramatic and life-altering revelation."

"How do you think people would react?"

"Reactions would probably vary. Some might be fascinated and curious, while others might feel fear and discomfort. If it becomes widely known and accepted that intelligent extraterrestrial life exists, I think it would cause deep philosophical and religious implications. Religious groups, especially those that interpret their scriptures literally, might react in ways that could create problems."

"How so?"

"Maybe with shock, denial, and distrust in society at large? Who knows? Hopefully, the discovery will bring humanity together even more, with a renewed drive to combat global warming."

"Did you hesitate to tell me all this?"

"Yes, absolutely. If we weren't in this situation, where we're not sure if we'll ever get out, I probably wouldn't have shared this with anyone. Not even you, Rashid."

CHAPTER 18

"Fredrik, you've mentioned before that there have been numerous climate-related disasters around the world with extremely high death tolls. You also said the UN has grown stronger and is now primarily focused on managing global climate issues. How's it going? Have they managed to reverse the negative trends? Is there hope? What actions have they taken?"

> "The short answer is that a lot has been done, but the situation is still incredibly serious. The global average temperature continues to rise, sea levels are climbing, polar ice caps and glaciers are shrinking, mass extinctions continue, extreme weather events are more frequent, and new diseases triggered by climate change keep appearing. One of the biggest threats near us right now is that there are signs the Gulf Stream is significantly weakening and might even collapse. This could lead to dramatic climate shifts in Europe within a short time, causing massive refugee crises. For example, Sweden and the other Scandinavian countries could end up with a climate similar to Alaska's."

"Isn't there anything positive to say about the climate?"

"There is; the rate of increase in Earth's average temperature is slowing down, the curves aren't rising as sharply as they once did. The measures to slow down climate change are beginning to have an effect."

"What measures?"

"I think I've mentioned some of them before, haven't I?"

"It's fine if you repeat some of what you said earlier."

"Okay, I'll try. The UN is working on multiple fronts simultaneously. One major role is to provide immediate disaster relief whenever something serious happens anywhere in the world. Unfortunately, climate change has made disasters more frequent. I think they've developed a strong, very effective organization for this. Resources once used to handle wars and conflicts are now focused on this type of disaster relief. They can often quickly rebuild damaged infrastructure, deliver supplies, provide medical care, construct temporary housing and hospitals, and manage the refugee flows that often result from these catastrophes."

"That's great, but that's more about dealing with the aftermath. What are they doing to prevent these situations?"

"Another crucial role for the UN is to prevent serious international conflicts from arising, to act proactively, in other words. The world can't afford to waste resources on wars and other types of armed conflict; every available resource must go toward tackling climate problems."

"Please, tell me more."

"I think I mentioned earlier that when there's a dispute over ownership or control of a land area, the UN's main principle is to temporarily classify it as an international zone under UN control and protection. They aim to prevent anything that could escalate into warfare as early as possible."

"Yes, you mentioned that before."

"Another conflict-dampening and conflict-preventing task for the UN is to address historical injustices. The countries that historically had, and still largely have, the most wealth are also those primarily responsible for global warming. Therefore, it's only fair that the wealthiest part of the world bears most of the costs of dealing with climate change's negative effects and investing in new solutions. Ignoring this principle would undoubtedly pave the way for future conflicts. The AI-based prediction tools, the so-called future simulators, are very clear on this point."

"That also sounds very sensible."

"The UN also applies the principles of shared international ownership of natural resources and other limited resources. These resources are considered internationally owned and protected by the UN, which then distributes them as fairly as possible."

"That sounds complicated. Does this happen without some countries feeling disadvantaged or previous resource owners feeling deprived?"

"It's worked surprisingly smoothly. Let me try to explain how resource-sharing works with an example, if you'd like?"

"Yes, please do."

"Hydrogen has become the main fuel for almost all types of transportation, including air, sea, and road travel. It's great because hydrogen emissions are just water."

"Okay, but where does all the hydrogen come from?"

"That's what I was getting to. Large amounts of electricity are needed to produce hydrogen. In the past, fossil fuels like coal, oil, and gas were often used to generate that electricity, but all those fuels have been banned by the UN since they contributed significantly to global warming. Today, electricity comes from sources like solar panels, wind turbines, hydroelectric power from rivers and tidal currents, and even nuclear power."

"Nuclear power? Isn't that problematic?"

"Both yes and no. A large portion of the electricity used to make hydrogen comes from several very large nuclear plants scattered worldwide. All these facilities are now international property, owned by everyone through the UN. The areas where the plants are located are classified as international territory. Since the uranium fuel for these plants is a limited resource and requires careful handling, the mines where it's extracted are also international territory. The UN operates these plants, guards and protects these areas, and distributes the hydrogen based on factors like population and the energy needs of each country's geographical location."

"How is the hydrogen transported to end-users?"

"Most of these nuclear plants are large floating facilities at sea, and from there, hydrogen is transported by massive tankers to different users."

"And these tankers are probably hydrogen-powered too."

"Naturally. The ports at these floating nuclear facilities also serve as refueling stations for other ships."

"What about the waste from the nuclear plants?"

"Good question, I was just about to explain. Yes, waste handling is also under UN control. Both the fuel and the waste could theoretically be used by malicious powers to make nuclear weapons, so it's essential that the entire lifecycle is managed responsibly."

"Aren't there already a huge number of nuclear weapons around the world? Doesn't that pose a big threat?"

"There were a lot, but they've all been dismantled. That disarmament is seen as one of the UN's most significant achievements."

"How did they manage that?"

"We, meaning the world, have come terrifyingly close to a devastating third world war a few times. Analyses of these instances showed that both tactical and strategic nuclear weapons were moments away from being used. Simulations showed that if we hadn't managed to avert these crises, more than half of the world's population would likely have died within months, either directly or indirectly. Once these analyses became public and were widely accepted as credible, it wasn't difficult for the UN to push for disarmament. Even though a few country leaders wanted to keep some nuclear weapons for *balance of terror*, the public pressure worldwide was so intense that keeping these weapons became impossible."

"What about all the smaller nuclear power plants around the world?"

"Almost all have been phased out. Some larger facilities have been incorporated into the internationally owned and UN-controlled system. For security and control reasons, the UN doesn't want many smaller plants owned by individual countries or corporations."

"What about everything else that contributed to global warming? What actions have been taken there? Do we still have any rainforests left?"

"In terms of deforestation, they've been fairly successful in stopping it, but as with everything else, these efforts should have been bigger and started earlier. Since rainforest areas are vital to the entire planet, large parts of them have now been protected by the UN, including most of what's left of the Amazon. The rainforests act as *the lungs of the Earth* and are essential for biodiversity. Locals in and near protected rainforest areas now receive economic support through the UN to leave the forests untouched. Many are also working on replanting vegetation that's especially good at capturing carbon dioxide."

"What about the environmental impacts of food production? Doesn't that still cause a lot of harmful emissions?"

"Historically, food production has indeed resulted in large greenhouse gas emissions."

"How so?"

"Partly from deforestation to create farmland and pasture, the use of artificial fertilizers, fossil fuels for farming equipment and fishing boats, and methane emissions from livestock when they burp and pass gas."

"How do you know so much about that?"

"As a journalist, I did a report on these issues years ago."

"Isn't food production still a major emitter of greenhouse gases?"

"No, things are pretty different now. It no longer causes such large emissions. Machines and transportation run on electricity or hydrogen. New crops have been developed to yield better harvests, withstand warmer climates, and don't require artificial fertilizers. Gene editing technology has revolutionized food production. AI-based decision support and various types of robots have made everything far more efficient than before."

"But livestock still burp and pass gas, right?"

"Even that problem is almost gone. Using gene editing, they've developed feed and livestock breeds that emit barely any greenhouse gases."

"Are both the feed and the animals genetically modified?"

"Yes."

"Isn't that risky and ethically controversial?"

"It was at first, but not anymore. Humanity has been selectively breeding plants and animals for thousands of years. Creating new plants and animal breeds isn't new. With modern gene editing technology and AI support, we're doing the same thing, but with greater precision and much faster."

"Can't it go wrong? Isn't it risky?"

"Sure, but since humanity has caused so much damage, resulting in global warming that severely threatens our existence, we unfortunately have to accept these risks if we want a chance to repair the damage. One of the most exciting and hopeful gene editing projects underway right now is creating a tree that's extremely good at capturing carbon dioxide from the atmosphere. The scientists working on this believe they'll succeed in just a few years."

"I read a scary book once where a malicious power created genetically engineered soldiers who were super strong, couldn't feel pain, and lacked emotions. The idea was to create an invincible army. Couldn't gene editing create those kinds of risks?"

"The risk exists, but all gene editing activities are regulated by UN agencies and must follow ethical guidelines set by the UN."

"Isn't there too much trust in the UN? Don't you yourself have too much faith in this organization?"

"What's the alternative? The UN is democratically run by the world's countries, which are now all democratic. All UN activities are completely transparent, there are supposed to be no secrets or hidden groups within the UN."

"Do you really trust that?"

"Yes, 99 percent. And since everything is constantly scrutinized and questioned within the democratic system, I believe any irregularities would quickly come to light and be addressed."

"Have there been any irregularities found in recent years? You said you trust the organization 99 percent ... so not entirely, not 100 percent."

"Yes, of course, nothing is perfect, but so far, I think the UN has worked excellently. I don't think there's a better alternative. Do you?"

"I haven't thought it through. A super-smart, super-kind AI system that's superior to humans in its thinking ability, could that be an alternative? Maybe such a system should have ultimate power?"

"No way! You've probably read a little too much science fiction?"

"There's one area that generates a lot of emissions that you haven't talked about yet."

"Which one?"

"Buildings. A lot of energy goes into heating or cooling buildings. Doesn't that still generate a lot of greenhouse gases?"

"That was true in the past, but since coal, oil, and gas use is banned and has been replaced with other energy sources, those issues have nearly vanished. The electricity we use is generated in climate-friendly ways, as we discussed earlier, right?"

"Yes, yes ... that's true."

"Major improvements have also been made in urban planning."

"How so?"

"The principle of the so-called '*15-minute city*' has globally gained widespread acceptance. Cities, neighborhoods, and communities are designed so that almost everything you need is within a 15-minute walk or bike ride. Jobs, schools, stores, healthcare, and all kinds of services should be easily and environmentally accessed within 15 minutes by foot or bike."

"Nice."

"They've also been mindful of geographic placement for new cities, trying as much as possible to put them in '*naturally air-conditioned*' areas, not places that are sometimes extremely hot or cold. Because of rising sea levels, millions of people have had to relocate to new areas, and they've taken the opportunity to place these new communities in low-energy-demand regions. In some cases, when coastal areas had to be abandoned, they've solved the problem by creating floating cities in the form of artificial islands."

"Oh, so people can still live close to where they used to live."

"Sometimes, yes. There are even a few examples where these artificial islands move slowly with the seasons, keeping a pleasant climate year-round. It does take some energy to move these cities, but they save a lot of energy with reduced heating and cooling needs. The nearby urban farms also benefit from better growing conditions."

"Sara told me about some retired relatives of hers who used to live in Sweden during the summer and in Spain during the winter, so they always had a comfortable climate. This sounds like something similar."

"Yes, but today's '*island nomads*' bring their homes, jobs, schools, and services along with them."

"That sounds both smart and comfortable."

CHAPTER 19

"Fredrik, there's something I'd like to talk to you about."

"What? It sounds serious."

"It's a trivial thing ... but I feel bad about it?"

"I think I know what you're about to say ... you've got stomach issues."

"How did you know?"

"When you live as close as we do now, you can't hide a bad stomach."

"Sorry."

"No need to apologize. My stomach's out of whack too. You might've noticed we're almost out of toilet paper?"

"Is it the dog food? Maybe our one-sided diet isn't that great."

"I think it's more likely the water. I feel like the taste has worsened, and it's started to smell a bit weird."

"I've noticed the water tastes different too, but I thought it was just my imagination."

"If the water keeps getting worse, we might need to try and get out of here. Without access to water or any other liquid, we'd die in just a few days, right?"

"It feels like our situation just got much more serious. Water is really important."

"Yeah, when I talked about how the UN handles conflicts over limited resources, I probably should've used water as an example. Water scarcity worldwide has been and still is the leading cause of conflicts and disasters. The UN has had to intervene in numerous water-related conflicts around the world."

"How so?"

"A number of major freshwater sources, both above and below ground, have become international zones where the critical water is distributed fairly based on various countries' needs."

"Are there certain lakes that have become international?"

"It's both lakes and river basins, as well as significant groundwater reservoirs. An individual country can no longer take control of any of these crucial freshwater resources for its own selfish purposes."

"Has that been a problem before? Have some countries taken too much?"

"Yes! Many rivers flow through several countries, and there are historical examples of individual nations taking an unfairly large share of the water to irrigate their own regions. In some cases, rivers have even been redirected to keep as much as possible within a single country. Countries downstream have then faced enormous water supply issues."

"How selfish."

"Regarding large groundwater reservoirs deep in the ground, called aquifers, these can sometimes stretch across borders, spanning two or more countries. It's unreasonable for one country to take most of the water and cause issues for other nations. In some places, such conflict zones, or potential conflict zones, have also become international, and the UN ensures these limited resources are distributed fairly. We also need to consider the needs of future generations."

"Have they come up with good ways to desalinate seawater?"

"Oh, yes, but it takes an enormous amount of energy. Some major desalination plants used to create fresh water are also now under UN control. The large floating nuclear power facilities I mentioned before often produce both hydrogen and drinking water."

"But what about our tricky water situation here? Has it gotten to the point where we should try to get out?"

"I'm not sure. Maybe we should stockpile some water in case the quality continues to worsen?"

"Do we have any containers for that?"

"Do you think the tank in the room that may have been a pantry could work?"

"Maybe, but how would we get water into the tank, and is it clean enough inside?"

"I've got it! The waste barrels!"

"The barrels in the bathroom? The spare toilets?"

"Yes, I checked those barrels earlier; they're stacked three high. I think there are eight sets of three each, so we have 24 barrels, each holding around 20-30 liters."

"That's a lot of liters."

"Yes, and there were also some plastic lids for the barrels."

"I hope none of the barrels were used."

"I don't think so. The ones I checked only smelled a bit like plastic."

"How are we going to get the water into the barrels? Scooping it one mug at a time will take forever."

"I have an idea ... the vacuum hose! If we put the barrels in the kitchen, we could guide the water from the faucet into one barrel at a time using the vacuum hose."

"Smart!"

"There might be a downside to this ... "

"What's that?"

"If we take a lot of water in a short period, it might make the water quality worsen even faster. What if there's some kind of purification or filtration system that only works well with moderate use and can't handle a high demand quickly? We don't want to speed up the water's deterioration."

"Oh, I hadn't thought of that. Maybe we should think this through before starting."

"I wonder how clean or dirty a vacuum hose is on the inside."

"There's a lot to consider."

"Sounds like it's time for a thinking break. Let's lie down for a bit and weigh the pros and cons before making a decision."

"Good idea, but first, I need to go to the bathroom. Is that okay?"

"Sure, but don't take too long, I need to go soon too."

CHAPTER 20

"Quiet, Fredrik!"

"What's wrong with you? What do you mean? I haven't said anything."

"Didn't you notice?"

"Notice what?"

"The ventilation stopped. That faint hum is gone. I don't feel any air coming out of the vent above the door."

"Are we going to die now? Do you think this is the end?"

"I don't know, but it feels very unsettling."

"I feel like the air's already getting a little worse."

"Already? So fast? That could be psychological, making you think so. The silence might be tricking your senses."

"Rashid, what if this silence now gives us a chance to make contact with someone up there, if anyone alive is still out there?"

"What do you mean? Should we scream, '*Help, can you hear us*'?"

"No, no, that probably wouldn't work ... but if the ventilation pipes somehow lead to the outside world, we could tap on the pipes so it echoes up. SOS, isn't it three short taps followed by three long taps, and then three short taps again?"

"Okay, go ahead and tap if you think it might work."

"I want to try! I'll tap on the pipe now with this can; *'three short, three long, three short'*. Did you hear that? We got a response right away! Someone replied with the same signal!"

"Try a different message."

"Why? How? I don't know Morse code."

"Forget it, just try something!"

"Okay, but I don't get why. There! I wonder if what I just sent actually means anything."

"Listen!"

"This is insane! They responded with the exact same signal I tapped!"

"Didn't you notice how quickly they responded? Don't you get it?"

"Get what?"

"There's an echo effect in the ventilation system. It's your own signal, your message, bouncing back with a little delay."

"Sigh! I didn't think about that. Rashid, you just dashed my hopes. But I should've figured that out myself. How could I be so dumb?"

"It's typical human nature. Your strong desire to get the answer you hoped for made you less open to other explanations."

"Damn it!"

"Fredrik, now even I think the air's getting worse. It's starting to feel pretty stale."

"But we have the ventilation pump, the one with the handle. Should I start cranking it to try and get some fresh air?"

"Yes! Do it, do it right away! Hurry up, and then we'll take turns cranking."

"I'm on it."

"Let me know when you want a break."

"I'm cranking as hard as I can, but it's just blowing stale air right in my face. Is it supposed to be like this?"

"I don't think so. I'm coming."

"Is something wrong?"

"Oh my God! Bad news, really bad news. Feel this, the pump isn't connected to the ventilation pipe at all. It's hanging loose next to it. How did we not notice this before?"

"Is this the moment we should try to get out of here?"

"Yeah, it's probably time; the air's only getting worse."

"Which of the two doors should we try to get out through? The one with the long handles or the one with the hand-wheels?"

"Wait! Do you hear that? There's a strange sound ... where's it coming from?"

"I hear it now. It's coming from over here, behind the door with the hand-wheels. Come here! Put your ear to the door. Listen."

"It sounds like some kind of machine ... that low hum and faint whine."

"Now it's getting a little louder, like it's coming closer. Should we bang on the door to let them know we're here? Should we open the door? Should we yell something?"

"What do you think?"

"I don't know."

"Listen! Now the sound's getting a little quieter ... maybe they're already moving away."

"You think?"

"Now it's even fainter! They're leaving! We have to let them know we're here!"

"You're right. I agree, and the air is getting really bad now. Hello, hello!"

"Fredrik, help me bang on the door. Hello! Can you hear us?"

"We need to open it now! I'll turn the upper hand-wheel, and you can take the lower one."

"I can't turn it; it's stuck. It doesn't move at all."

"Move over and let me try. Oh, come on! Damn thing, move!"

"Are you turning it the right way?"

"It should be the same direction as the upper hand-wheel, but I've tried both ways. Help me; let's try together."

"It won't move a millimeter."

"A lever would help if we could wedge it between the spokes. Can you get a chair? The chair leg might work as a lever. Hurry; the air's getting worse by the second."

"Here, Fredrik, here's the chair."

"Geez, this thing's on so tight, the chair leg is bending, but the hand-wheel won't move."

"Try this. I managed to snap a leg off the table in the meeting room. It's a strong metal bar."

"Thanks, Rashid! Now this hand-wheel should start turning. Help me, grab here below my hands so we can both press down."

"Okay!"

"Now! Now! Now!"

"It's not working!"

"Step aside; I'll try stomping on the bar."

"Go ahead!"

"Damn it! This thing is like a rock."

"What do we do now? Why is the air getting worse so fast? I'm finding it harder and harder to breathe. We need to get out!"

"Should we try the other door?"

"Wait, do you hear that? The sound's getting closer again. I think they might have heard us."

"Bang on the door! Where's the can?"

"Here, take it. Pound hard against the door. Bang, bang! Hello, hello!"

"I think they're right outside ... it sounds like they're right there ... on the other side of the door. Hello!"

"Why aren't they answering? Can they not hear us, or do they not want to respond?"

"I don't know."

"Now it sounds different! Do you hear that? It sounds like they're trying to cut or drill through the door. Whoa, it's vibrating. Don't stand too close!"

"Rashid, this might be the end for us."

"It might also be the beginning of a new chapter in our lives."

"This feels scary. I'm terrified! I'm really scared! I'm scared as hell!"

"Me too, but we don't know for sure; this could also be our rescue, right?"

"Whatever happens, it was a privilege, an honor to get to know you, Rashid. You're an amazing person."

"You too, Fredrik. Can I hug you?"

"Of course!"

"Do you hear that? They're almost through!"

"Yeah, they're really close now. I'm scared!"

"Why didn't they answer when we called out and banged?"

"I don't know. Whatever or whoever is on the other side might not have wanted to, or been able to respond, maybe not even capable of it."

"Whatever or whoever? Who could it be? What could it be?"

"Well, we might soon find out what's on the other side."

"Is this the end?"

CHAPTER 21

"Rashid, how are you? Are you awake?"

"I don't know. My body feels numb. I can barely lift a finger. Am I dreaming, or am I awake?"

"Why do you think you could be dreaming?"

"I'm lying in a bed with sheets. There's no bubble wrap. Where am I? I'm not still in the bunker, right, Fredrik? The sounds, the acoustics of the room are different too."

"You're lying in a bed at Östersund Hospital. They kept you sedated for a little over three weeks so your body could have a chance to recover. That's why you feel so tired and weak. That's also why you have all these wires and tubes connected to you."

"Three weeks! Recover from what?"

"Your body was badly injured when the door exploded, and you went through multiple surgeries. You were standing way too close, but the doctors say you'll fully recover from the injuries caused by the blast."

"Why didn't they tell us to stand back from the door? You and I were shouting and banging, so they must have heard us. Didn't they know we were on the other side?"

"The fully autonomous robot that breached the door with cutting tools and explosives didn't have the ability to listen. That function was missing. The robot was simply instructed to get through the door."

"What about you, Fredrik, were you injured too?"

"No, I made it out by sheer luck. I was feeling so sick to my stomach that I had just rushed to the bathroom right before the blast. It was nerve-wracking running back after hearing the explosion and feeling my way to find you lying there silently, badly hurt among the debris. Luckily, a few people arrived soon after to give you first aid, and they had flashlights so they could see what they were doing. They also made sure you were quickly taken to the hospital."

"Didn't they know we were down there in the bunker? Why did they wait so long to try to get us out?"

"Yes, they knew we were down there, but they were convinced we were dead, that we had probably died soon after arriving. There were apparently motion sensors down there, as well as sensors that measured things like oxygen and carbon dioxide levels, and these showed no signs that either of us was alive."

"They thought we were done for?"

"Yes! Other sensors indicated the environment was lethally dangerous in various ways. That's why they waited. However, they hadn't realized that all these sensors were placed inside the old weapons lab, behind a bricked-up door. They'd set up the sensors there to monitor that extremely hazardous environment. Apparently, the old weapons lab had a power source that kept the sensors running."

"So, there was functional electricity right near us, behind a sealed door."

"Sara told me she was devastated when she was informed we couldn't possibly be alive. She thought she'd sent us to our deaths by forcing us into the elevator."

"So, Sara's alive! That's wonderful! What caused the strange flash of light, then?"

"It turned out to be an old Chinese research satellite burning up when it re-entered Earth's atmosphere."

"So, we probably would've been safe if we'd stayed up top?"

"Yes, we would've been, but Sara didn't know that when she pushed us into the elevator."

"You said my body was severely injured by the explosion, but I don't feel any pain."

"The staff here at the hospital are extremely skilled at pain management."

"How much longer will I be here? Will they be sending me back to the facility soon?"

"No, you won't be going back. With the help of a lawyer, I've already managed to get an emergency court ruling that you're to be released as soon as possible. They'll also arrange a place for you to live and make sure you get the support you need to re-enter society. If you want, you can also stay with me for a while."

"Thank you, Fredrik, that's incredibly kind, but how long do you think I'll need to stay here in the hospital?"

"I don't know. It'll probably take several weeks before you regain your strength. Unfortunately, both of your kidneys were severely damaged in the explosion, so you're currently on daily dialysis."

"So, I might never fully recover?"

"Oh, yes, you will! They say you'll get either an artificial kidney or a transplant."

"Do you really think there's someone willing to donate a kidney to me?"

"Definitely! I know there is, and it's someone very special."

"What do you mean?"

"Through the international donation registry and using your DNA, the hospital has already found a woman in Norway who's a perfect match. She's in her 30s."

"A perfect match in Norway? How come?"

"Rashid, try to stay calm. What I'm about to tell you will probably seem both shocking and wonderful."

"Tell me!"

"This potential donor originally came from Afghanistan and moved to Norway when she was about eight years old. A Norwegian medical team saved her life after someone brought her into their field hospital. She'd been found in a deep ravine, badly injured from some sort of external trauma, and extremely dehydrated. After receiving emergency care, she was flown to Norway, where she underwent several successful surgeries. Once she recovered, she was adopted by a Norwegian family, as she was considered an orphan."

"Why do they think she's a perfect donor for me? Is it just because she's from Afghanistan?"

"It's actually far more perfect than that, DNA tests show that you're related. You're even close family. She's your younger sister. It's Samira!"

"That can't be true! My God! Is it really Samira? Is it really her? She's alive?"

"Yes, the DNA analysis confirmed one hundred percent that you're siblings."

"I think I'm going to pass out. Such joy, such happiness. Is this really true?"

"Yes, it's true, and I've already spoken to her. She's now fully convinced that you're siblings, and she absolutely wants to donate a kidney. She's also eager to meet you."

"I don't know if I can handle this. This is pure happiness!"

"There's more. Samira, who also goes by the name Stine now, is married to a man named Reidar. They have two children together, a daughter named Nora, who's four, and a son named Henrik, who's two."

"So, I'm an uncle now too. That's amazing!"

"You might want to consider that eye surgery to restore your vision. The kids are adorable."

"What? Have you seen them?"

"Yes, your sister sent me a picture."

"I'm so happy. Thank you, Fredrik. When can I meet Samira and her family?"

"You'll probably need to wait a few weeks until you're stronger."

"Fredrik, have you heard from Dolores?"

"Of course! As soon as I got out of the underground bunker, I contacted her. She'd been worried since she hadn't heard from me in several days and was scared I didn't want to keep in touch."

"But you do, of course."

"Yes, and now I've also booked a flight to Hawaii. I'm leaving early next week."

"Even though it's so expensive to fly?"

"Yes, it's costly, really costly, but the flight has to be fossil-free."

"What made you finally book that trip?"

"There are two reasons. First, I felt like I just had to see Dolores as soon as possible. Plus, she wants me there by the end of next week."

"Why then?"

"Her team will be holding a press conference to announce a groundbreaking astronomical discovery. Dolores really wants me to be there for it."

"I think I know what it's about."

"Rashid, you must not tell anyone else about the discoveries Dolores' team has made."

"I promise!"

"Thank you, Rashid. I know I can trust you."

"I also have to say thank you, Fredrik. You have given me hope for a better tomorrow."